Some troubles come along
when you need them the least.

Some books come along when
you need them the most.

Here's a book especially for you...
       to encourage you on
          and to help you
             hang in there.

Also by Douglas Pagels

Chasing Away the Clouds

*Every Daughter Should Have
a Book like This*

*For You, Just Because
You're Very Special to Me*

I Want You to Read This Today...

A Keepsake for My Children

100 Things to Always Remember...

Required Reading for All Teenagers

*30 Beautiful Things
That Are True About You*

*To the One Person I Consider to Be
My Soul Mate*

All writings are by Douglas Pagels except as noted.

Library of Congress Control Number: 2005905272
ISBN: 1-59842-111-5

Certain trademarks are used under license.
BLUE MOUNTAIN PRESS is registered in U.S. Patent and Trademark Office.

Acknowledgments appear on page 4.

Manufactured in the United States of America.
First Printing: 2005

 This book is printed on recycled paper.

This book is printed on fine quality, laid embossed, 80 lb. paper. This paper has been specially produced to be acid free (neutral pH) and contains no groundwood or unbleached pulp. It conforms with the requirements of the American National Standards Institute, Inc., so as to ensure that this book will last and be enjoyed by future generations.

Blue Mountain Arts, Inc.

P.O. Box 4549, Boulder, Colorado 80306

Everyone
should have
a book
like this
to get
through the
gray days

Douglas Pagels

Blue Mountain Press ™

Boulder, Colorado

ACKNOWLEDGMENTS

We gratefully acknowledge the permission granted by the following authors, publishers, and authors' representatives to reprint poems or excerpts from their publications.

Hay House, Inc., Carlsbad, CA, for "Sometimes success is just a matter..." from LIFE LESSONS AND REFLECTIONS by Montel Williams. Copyright © 2000 by Montel Williams. All rights reserved.

G.P. Putnam's Sons, a division of Penguin Group (USA), Inc., for "I wake up every day with..." from A LOTUS GROWS IN THE MUD by Goldie Hawn. Copyright © 2005 by Illume, LLC. All rights reserved.

Hyperion for "I'm dealing with it my own..." from DOWN CAME THE RAIN by Brooke Shields. Copyright © 2005 by Christa Incorporated. All rights reserved. And for "Luck plays a part in everybody's..." from THE WINNING ATTITUDE! by Michelle Kwan. Copyright © 1999 by Michelle Kwan Corp. All rights reserved. And for "What matters in the end..." by Ann Curry from AL ROKER & HIS FRIENDS by Al Roker. Copyright © 2005 by Al Roker. All rights reserved. Reprinted by permission of Hyperion.

Penguin Group (USA), Inc. for "When you think about it..." from IT'S NOT ABOUT THE BIKE by Lance Armstrong. Copyright © 2000, 2001 by Lance Armstrong. All rights reserved.

McGraw-Hill Education for "You can't turn back time..." from VENUS & SERENA: SERVING FROM THE HIP by Venus and Serena Williams. Copyright © 2005 by Venus Williams and Serena Williams. All rights reserved.

Dutton Children's Books, a Division of Penguin Young Readers Group, a Member of Penguin Group (USA), Inc., for "It's snowing still..." from WINNIE-THE-POOH by A. A. Milne. Illustrations by E. H. Shepard, copyright © 1928 by E. P. Dutton, renewed © 1956 by A. A. Milne. All rights reserved.

Bantam Books, a division of Random House, Inc., for "I know bad things can happen to..." from COMFORT FROM A COUNTRY QUILT by Reba McEntire. Copyright © 1999 by Reba McEntire. All rights reserved.

HarperResource, an imprint of HarperCollins Publishers, for "Now when I am beaten..." from IT'S NOT ABOUT THE BRA by Brandi Chastain. Copyright © 2004 by Brandi Chastain. All rights reserved.

A careful effort has been made to trace the ownership of selections used in this anthology in order to obtain permission to reprint copyrighted material and give proper credit to the copyright owners. If any error or omission has occurred, it is completely inadvertent, and we would like to make corrections in future editions provided that written notification is made to the publisher:

BLUE MOUNTAIN ARTS, INC., P.O. Box 4549, Boulder, Colorado 80306.

Contents

Remember What
Reinhold Said...

God grant me
the serenity to
accept the things
I cannot change;
the courage to
change the things
I can; and the
wisdom to know
the difference.

— Reinhold Niebuhr

It's going to be okay.

Just give things a little time.
And in the meantime...
keep believing in yourself;
take the best of care;
try to put things in perspective;
remember what's most important;
don't forget that someone cares;
search for the positive side;
learn the lessons to be learned;
and find your way through to
        the inner qualities...
    the strength, the smiles,
        the wisdom, and the
        optimistic outlook
    that are such special parts
    of you.

It's going to be okay.

    You're going to make it
    through the gray days.

Hang In There & Keep Your Hopes Up

Difficulties arise in the lives of us all. What is most important is dealing with the hard times, coping with the changes, and getting through to the other side where the sun is still shining just for you.

It takes a strong person to deal with tough times and difficult choices. But you are a strong person. It takes courage. But you possess the inner courage to see you through. It takes being an active participant in your life. But you are in the driver's seat, and you can determine the direction you want tomorrow to go in.

Take care to see that you don't lose sight of the one thing that is constant, beautiful, and true: Everything will be fine — and it will turn out that way because of the special kind of person you are.

So... beginning today and lasting a lifetime through — hang in there, and don't be afraid to feel like the morning sun is shining... just for you.

If I could have any wish I wanted,
   this is my wish...

That in your life,
   which is so precious to me,
may troubles, worries, and problems
never linger;
may they only make you
that much stronger and able
and wise.

And may you rise each day with
sunlight in your heart,
success in your path,
answers to your prayers, and
that smile — that I love to see —
      always there... in your eyes.

Remember What
Montel Said...

Sometimes success
is just a matter
of hanging on.

— Montel Williams

A Little Prayer
I'd Love to Share
with You

I want your life to be
such a wonderful one.
I wish you peace. Deep within
your soul.
Joyfulness. In the promise of
each new day.
Stars. To reach for. Dreams.
To come true.
Memories. More beautiful
than words can say.

I wish you friends. Close at heart,
even over the miles.
Loved ones. The best treasures
we're blessed with...

Present moments. To live in,
 one day at a time.
Serenity. With its wisdom.
Courage. With its strength.
New beginnings. To give life a
 chance to really shine.

I wish you understanding. Of how
 special you really are.
A journey. Safe from the storms
 and warmed by the sun.
A path. To wonderful things.
An invitation. To the abundance
 life brings.
And an angel watching over.
 For all the days to come.

Remember What Goldie Said...

I wake up every day with the intention to be loving and happy and the best I can be. I try to make each day a new day without carrying over the baggage from the previous day.

— Goldie Hawn

Living in the past is hard work.

There can be way too much baggage to take along, and it can drag you down to the point where it's difficult to see things from the right perspective. It's better to stay light on your feet, bright in your outlook, and easy on yourself.

Living in the future?

That's no walk in the park either. Some people who live in the future spend all their time getting carried away with worry and anxiety — and stressing out over the worst that could conceivably come true. They're like passengers who are so busy standing by the lifeboats that they completely miss out on the fun of the cruise.

The real gift?

It's the one we're given every day... to open, to use any way we want, to grow, to get better, to share with others, and to treasure so completely.

What a wonderful present.

A Gentle Reminder for a Wonderful Person Living in a Difficult World

The hard times of life
can be overwhelming.
I'm not here to tell you that
things will be perfect tomorrow or
even next week... because they won't be.
They'll be different and sometimes
they'll be demanding.

But I am here to tell you
that you will get through this.
I'm absolutely, positively sure you
will. Everything will be fine.

Everyone who cares about you
will be here to help. And
the passage of time will be
one of the friends who will
see you through this journey.

Little by little, things will be better.
The sun is still shining up above,
and it's going to do whatever it can
to peek through the clouds and
sneak in your kitchen window and
brighten up your life once again.

And as the days go by, lots of other
things will ask if they can join in:
inner strength, increasing confidence,
a better perspective, and peace of mind.
And someday soon I think you'll find:
 It's not the end of the world.

 Sometimes it's the start...
  of a brand-new beginning.

Here is some gentle wisdom
that will get you through just
about anything:

Appreciate, with all your heart,
   the best of life.
Do everything within your power
   to pass the tests of life.
And learn how to live
      with the rest of life.

Remember What
Brooke Said...

I'm dealing with
it my own way.
One thing
at a time.

— Brooke Shields

One Day at a Time

I have learned that the best way to deal with difficulties, to get through times of sadness, to handle stress, and to make definite progress, is to break time down into increments that our hearts and our comfort zones can handle.

For most things that life can throw our way, we can make it through a day at a time. The hours of that one day are the only parameters we're dealing with here. The concerns of yesterday are things of the past. And we'll cross tomorrow's bridge when we come to it… but not before. But today? Today is okay. It's here and it's now. It's a period of time that we can see and feel and manage and give meaning to. We can recognize the gift that it is and make the most of the present moment.

Living life a day at a time means living a life that is blessed with awareness, appreciation, and accomplishment. For one day, you can be everything you were meant to be. You can be as strong as you need to be.

For one amazing day…

The weight is lifted. The path is clearer.
The goal is attainable. The prayer is heard.
The strength is sure. The courage is complete.
The belief is steady and sweet and true.

For one remarkable day…

There is a brighter light in your life. The will
to walk up the mountain takes you exactly
where you want to go. The heart understands
what serenity really means. And your hopes
and wishes and dreams will not disappear
from view.

For one magnificent day…

You can live with an abundance of love and
goodness and grace shining inside of you.

For one very important day…

You can do
everything
you need to do.

Remember What This Says...

Life is not measured by the number of breaths we take, but by the moments that take our breath away.

— Anonymous

You are so deserving of every good thing that can come your way. And I want you to know, if I could have a wish come true, I'd wish for every day of your life to be blessed with some special gift that warms your heart, some wonderful smile that
touches your soul,
and so many things that simply take your breath away.

May You Always Have
an Angel by Your Side

May you always have an angel by your
side ⁊ Watching out for you in all the things
you do ⁊ Reminding you to keep believing in
brighter days ⁊ Finding ways for your wishes
and dreams to take you to beautiful places ⁊
Giving you hope that is as certain as the
sun ⁊ Giving you the strength of serenity as
your guide ⁊ May you always have love and
comfort and courage ⁊ And may you always
have an angel by your side ⁊

May you always have an angel by your side ⁊
Someone there to catch you if you fall ⁊
Encouraging your dreams ⁊ Inspiring your
happiness ⁊ Holding your hand and helping
you through it all ⁊

In all our days, our lives are always changing ✶
Tears come along as well as smiles ✶ Along the
roads you travel, may the miles be a thousand
times more lovely than lonely ✶ May they give
you gifts that never, ever end: someone
wonderful to love and a dear friend in whom
you can confide ✶ May you have rainbows after
every storm ✶ May you have hopes to keep
you warm ✶

✶ And may you always have an angel
by your side ✶

Would you like to know something really wonderful about you?

You can do just about anything you want... if you put your mind to it. And you know that it's easy to invest in the best riches of all. That precious moments are most likely to come to those who search them out. That cherished times are to be found in all the things you do that strengthen your spirit and bring you a smile that stays in your life.

You can move ahead of any worries, move beyond any sorrows, and give yourself an opportunity to make your own special story... almost anything you want it to be.

A new part of your life is just waiting for you. It's filled with new chapters and unread pages. It's filled with hope from cover to cover... and it hopes you will give it a chance to show you what it can do.

Remember What Lance Said...

When you think
about it,
what other choice
is there
but to hope?

— Lance Armstrong

When nothing is going right.
When you're wondering, "What
    did I do to deserve this?"
When the day is a disaster,
and a little serenity
    is just what you're after.
When you need a whole lot less
    to concern you,
and a whole lot more to smile about.
When a few peaceful hours
    would seem like a vacation to you,
and you're wondering if there's anything
    you've got to look forward to...

Sometimes you just have to remember:
　　It *really is* going to be okay.
　　You're going to make it
　　　　through this day.
　　Even if it's one step at a time.
Sometimes you just have to be
　　patient and brave and strong.
If you don't know how, just
　　make it up as you go along.
And hold on to your hope as though it
　　were a path to follow
　　　　or a song you love to sing.
Because if you have hope,
　　you have everything.

Remember What
Robert Said...

Don't spend your life brooding over sorrows and mistakes. Don't be the one who never gets over things.

— Robert Louis Stevenson

As the sun wakes up the world with its new hopes for happiness, may it shine on you and bring you the bright and beautiful gift that it so lovingly holds...

the gift of this special day.

May these moments unfold with peace, with promise, with doors that open on new beginnings and windows that look out on a world filled with wishes waiting to come true.

And as this day comes full circle, may the quiet times of reflection bring an evening of serenity, may a distant star find you, and may it remind you that you're someone very special...

someone who is going to make it through every gray day that comes along.

Don't Ever Stop
Dreaming Your Dreams

Don't ever try to understand everything —
some things will just never make sense.
Don't ever be reluctant
    to show your feelings —
    when you're happy, give in to it!
    When you're not, live with it.
Don't ever be afraid to try to
    make things better —
    you might be surprised at the results.
Don't ever take the weight of the world
    on your shoulders.

Don't ever feel threatened by the future —
    take life one day at a time.
Don't ever feel guilty about the past —
    what's done is done. Learn from any
    mistakes you might have made.
Don't ever feel that you are alone —
    there is always somebody there for you
    to reach out to.
Don't ever forget that you can achieve
    so many of the things you can imagine —
    imagine that! It's not as hard as it seems.
Don't ever stop loving,
    don't ever stop believing,
        don't ever stop dreaming your dreams.

You need faith. That things will be better.
You need strength. And you'll find it within.
You need patience and persistence.
You need hope, and you need to keep it close
    to the center of everything that means the
    most to you.

You need to put things in perspective.
So much of your life lies ahead!
You need to know how good it can be.
You need to take the best of what you've
    learned from the old, and bring it to the
    beautiful days of a new journey.

Life's new beginnings happen for very
special reasons. When it's time to move on,
remember that it *really* is okay.
Because when a new beginning unfolds
in the story of your life, you go
    such a long way toward making
        the dreams of your tomorrows
            come true.

Remember What
Serena Said...

You can't turn back time…

If I'm not paying attention now because I'm thinking about something in the past, I won't make the right choices for my future. The best thing I can do is accept what has happened, quickly figure out what I need to do differently, make the change, and move on.

— Serena Williams

Nobody ever said that it would be easy, or that the skies would always be sunny. When gray days and worrisome times come along, you need to know that everything will turn out all right.

When life has got you down, remember: it's *okay* to feel vulnerable. You feel things deeply, and that is a wonderful quality to have. Rest assured that, in the long run, the good days will *far* outnumber the bad.

What is sometimes perceived as weakness is actually strength. The more you're bothered by something that's wrong, the more you're empowered to make things right.

If you have troubles, secrets you keep inside, problems that are getting to be more of a problem, and deep concerns...

You need to get help and learn the best way out and around and through. And you need to realize that you're not alone — other people are right there with you.

Happiness is waiting for you. Believe in your ability. Cross your bridges. Listen to your heart. Leave behind any little worries. Take the others *one at a time*, and you'll be amazed at how your difficulties manage to become easier.

Remember What
Eeyore Said...

It's snowing still.
And freezing.
However, we haven't
had an earthquake lately.

— Eeyore
From A. A. Milne's
House at Pooh Corner

I know this isn't earth-shaking news for you, but optimists have it *so much better* than their counterparts. I've known pessimistic people who, like Eeyore, never went anywhere without their own rain cloud following along. One fellow I knew expected the worst from everyone and everything. And more often than not, it seemed like that's what he got. With him, it wasn't a case of the glass being half-empty or half-full. It was a question of why bother putting *any* amount in the glass; it's eventually going to break anyway.

I'm sorry but... that kind of outlook is never going to work for me. I don't think it works for anyone. Given the choice, I'm going to keep the faith, fan the flames on every glimmer of hope, make plans for how I'll spend the brighter day that's on the way, laugh when I can, cry when I must, stay in touch with the people who truly matter, and keep on standing tall. I think if you do your best, the rest will take care of itself.

And I try to be optimistic... above all.

Choose Wisely

Decisions are incredibly important things!
Good decisions will come back to bless you.
Bad decisions can come back to haunt you.

That's why it's so important that you take the
time to choose wisely. Choose to do the things
that reflect well… on your ability, your integrity,
your spirit, your health, your tomorrows, your
smiles, your dreams, and yourself.

You are such a wonder. You're the only one in
the universe exactly like you! I want you to take
care of that rare and remarkable soul. I want you
to know that there is someone who will thank
you for doing the things you do now with
foresight and wisdom and respect.

It's the person you will someday be.

When you are feeling uncertain about what to do or which way to go, I want to gently remind you that so many days are filled with decisions... but if you let your heart help you decide what is right for you, I know you will choose wisely.

When you are in need of patience and faith and strength, I encourage you to rely on all the good things that would love to make themselves available to you:

inner peace, reaching out,
steady goals, staying strong,
and all your wonderful qualities
that have always seen you through
and that will continue to carry you on.

A Few Things
I Definitely Don't
Want You to Do

Don't stress out about things you have no
control over. Sometimes what is... just is.
Don't waste your days in emotional disarray
over a negative situation that you *can* be in
control of. Remember, you always have at
least three options: move on; stay where
you are and just deal with it; or turn a
difficult situation into a positive one.
Don't worry about your future. It will unfold
slowly enough and give you plenty of time to
decide... all the wheres and whens and whys.

Remember What William Said...

O Time, thou must
untangle this,
not I;

It is too hard a knot
for me to untie.

— William Shakespeare

It's About Time

There are times when life is so hard.

But when sad times or gray days come along, you need to stay strong, let time pass by, and try your best to put things in perspective.

The passage of time can work wonders. The closer you are to a crisis, the harder it is to realize how much easier things will eventually be. But it's absolutely true. The passage of time is precisely what it takes for so many essential things that will follow.

It takes time for the cycle of life to get back on track, for the days and nights to keep from getting turned around. It takes time for sleep to be easy and for the world to prove to you that your biggest fears aren't going to come true. It takes time to learn how to stay busy in a healthy way. It takes time to forget the pain and to put some much-needed distance between you and any difficult memories.

It takes time for comfort to settle in and for calls to come from family and friends who care about you and who want to share their love and kindness and support.

As the pages on the calendar continue to turn, you begin to realize that the world has been turning, too, and that things are different for you. More steady and serene. More of how you want things to be. One day you wake up and it feels like spring returning, like hope coming back after being gone too long. And it lets you see that, yes, life really does go on.

Eventually everything is going to be okay. I promise. You'll make progress. Things will balance themselves out. They always do.

Everyone says, "It just takes time." And you know what? Everyone's right.

Remember What
Michelle Said...

Luck plays a part in everybody's life. You always wish for the good kind, but — I hate to say it — somewhere along the line you'll run into the other kind. Even if you've got all the talent and desire and common sense in the world, life doesn't come with any guarantees. You can't take it back and trade it in for a new model. I just hope that your setbacks are small and that there's lots of space between them.

— Michelle Kwan

May life's little worries always stay small.
May you get a little closer, every day,
    to any goals you want to achieve.

May any changes be good ones,
    and any challenges turn out to be
    for the better.

May the days be good to you:
    comforting more often than crazy,
    and giving more often than taking.

May the passing seasons make sure that any
    heartaches are replaced with a million
    smiles, and that any hard journeys
    eventually turn into nice, easy miles
    that take you everywhere you want to go.

Keep Your Spirits Up

Keep focused. When one thing is wrong, it doesn't mean that everything is. It's easy to let yourself get overwhelmed, but try not to go there. If it's only one rock that is falling, don't let your worries turn it into a landslide.

Keep things in perspective. You've been through difficult times before. Think back on times when you wondered "How am I going to get through this?" And you know what? You always did. Just like you'll get through this.

Keep in mind that before too long, your gray days will be left behind, and your heart will guide you as you go.

On every step you take on your journey, all your inner strength, ability, and wisdom will walk along beside you, helping to carry you over any rough spots.

On every path you take beyond these tough times, you will be making transitions every step of the way. Every single day will get a little better. And as you travel along, toward all the special seasons of your life, I hope that you will be given every reason to believe that...

Whatever life lacks in preventing our sorrows,
it makes up for with
thousands of brighter tomorrows.

Worries & Concerns
(and things we eventually learn)

How are things going? Why is this happening? What could I have done differently? Have too many things been taken for granted? How can I change that? How can I make things turn out right? How can I help others? How can I help myself? What's it going to take? Where do I go from here?

There are so many questions in search of answers. And so many answers that are hard to hear when life is moving too fast. Slowing down lets us listen. One of the things it tells us is that positive results can come out of negative situations. And we need to keep the door open to that possibility. When there are difficult days...

There are more challenges, but also more chances, to truly understand the meaning of the moments and how your heart, your faith, and all the courage that it takes... figure into the plan.

Hard times sometimes make it easier for us
to really understand.

Remember What Reba Said...

I know bad things can happen to anyone, but I also know that I can't control that. All I can do is face whatever bad things happen with all the strength and courage I can summon from within so that I can go on with my life. That in itself is the hardest thing any of us will ever have to do, but we have to do it.

— Reba McEntire

(I can't stress this enough)
Try to Keep from Stressing Out

If you were to ask yourself — What do I want my life to be about? — I guarantee this: "Stress" has never been anyone's answer. It's such a destructive thing. A mild case of it can be unhealthy. A major case of it can be both physically and emotionally crippling. I've seen it happen firsthand, and I've come to understand how harmful it can be.

It's so sad when stress becomes part of our daily lives. Once in awhile, okay. That probably goes with the territory of living in this unpredictable world. But beyond that… it is not okay. When the warning signs start showing up everywhere, that's time to take heed, get help, and move on. There's a better way to live.

Part of the beauty of being a human being is this: you have options. You're a thinking, feeling, creative soul, and you can figure out how to be more in control of your own life. You're the author of this work, and you can make it work.

You can tackle stress and come out on top. You are capable. You have seen your way through many difficult things, and you can see your way through this. You can cope. You can handle the situation at hand.

You can hold on to your health, remembering that it is your ultimate compass, telling you if you're headed in the right direction or not.

You can seek out a place of serenity. You can even let yourself be selfish for a change. It's okay. Really. Instead of being the last one you take care of, remember that you can only share a smile if you've got one to share. Take the time to find yours again. If your stress is complicated by being a "Type A" personality, give yourself a break and see what it's like to be a different letter for a change... one that makes you happy and that greets you with a welcome-back smile when you see yourself in the mirror. Try to make sure that the person you see is a reflection... not of who you *have to* be... but who you *want to* be.

You can turn to friends and loved ones. You can talk it over 'till it's all talked out. You can look within, reach up, and have faith. You can make a plan, put it in place, and find the brighter day that's out there waiting for you. And most of all:

You can do it... because life is too short *not to*.

Remember What Brandi Said...

Now when I am beaten and disappointed and I sense my attitude is heading south, I think to myself, Deal with it, Brandi. Attitude is something we have control over, and that's my cue to regain a more positive frame of mind.

— Brandi Chastain

A Little Morale Booster

You're really something, do you know that? And in spite of whatever may happen in your day, you are going to stay that way: trying and giving and living life in the best way you know how. So keep your spirits up, and keep things in perspective. It's going to be okay.

You've made it through difficult things before, right? Right. And you always land on your feet. Maybe not dancing; maybe not always sure about what to do next. But you always manage to figure things out. Especially when you're able to keep your sense of humor and not lose your smile. If you really think about it, you'll realize that you are a very strong individual. Someone who may not have all the answers, but who is at least willing to hope and try and believe. You can see your way through just about anything; it all depends on how you look at it. And when I look at you, I see someone who really is... pretty amazing.

"Making That Positive Change"

Here's a goal for the day:

I'm going to take things one step at a time.
I will realize the worth of this moment
and the wonder of a new beginning.
I will remember what a treasure
I am holding in my hands, and I will say
a quiet thanks for the opportunity and
the promise... of this brand-new day.

Here's a motto for the week:

I will turn to the courage within me.
I will add richness to my life.
I will go without the things that should
be left behind, knowing that once those
anchors are no longer holding me down,
my spirit can lift me up so much easier...
    and I can rise above anything.
I can dream my dreams. I can do so much.
I can be someone I'm so proud of.

And here's a message for the month:

I will take all those positive steps, all those promises, and all those opportunities… and put them together into one great result. My heart will be so much fuller than it was just a month ago. My dreams will be a lot closer than they were only a few weeks ago. My confidence will just shine, because I will have spent the last 30 days polishing it up. I'll be looking at things from a brand-new point of view.

I'm a strong person. I'm a survivor. And I'm going to surprise a lot of people before I'm through. My progress will be obvious to everyone. But especially… to me.

And when I look in the mirror,
    nothing's going to be sweeter
    than smiling right back…
        at the wonderful person I see.

This Works Wonders

Sometimes it's important to work for that pot of gold. But other times it's essential to take time off and to make sure that your most important decision in the day simply consists of choosing which color to slide down on the rainbow.

Remember What
Ann Said...

What matters in the end
is what kind of person
you were. Did you do
your best, did you love
enough, were you
presented with a chance
to do good, did you
take it?

— Ann Curry

A Chance for a Happy Ending

We all know that life isn't easy.
If we could, we would just wave a magic
wand and make everything the way we
want it to be. We don't have that
luxury, but there are some things we
can do that will help to see us through.

We can have hope. Because it works
      wonders for those who have it.
We can be optimistic. Because every
      cloud does seem to have a silver lining.
We can put things in perspective.
      Because some things are important,
      and others are definitely not.

We can remember that beyond the
    clouds, the sun is still shining.
We can meet each challenge and give it
    all we've got.

We can count our blessings.
We can be inspired to climb our
    ladders to the stars.
We can be strong and patient.
We can be gentle and wise.

And we can believe in happy endings.
Because we are the authors of the
        stories of our lives.

And Remember
What I Said...

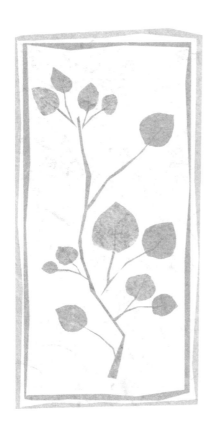

Count your blessings,
not your troubles.
You'll make it through
whatever comes along.
Within you are so many
answers. Understand,
have courage, be strong.

— Douglas Pagels

Tomorrow is a beautiful road that will take you right where you want to go...

If you spend today walking away from worry and moving toward serenity; leaving behind conflict and traveling toward solutions; and parting with emptiness and never giving up on your search for fulfillment. If you can do what works for you, your present will be happier and your path will be smoother. And best of all?

You'll be taking a step
    into a beautiful future.

About the Author

Bestselling author and editor Douglas Pagels has inspired millions of readers with his insights and anthologies. People of all ages and all walks of life are drawn to his work because they share so much with him: the same caring and concern, the same hopes and dreams, and so many of the same feelings. His writings have been translated into seven languages due to their global appeal and inspiring outlook on life, and his work has been quoted by many worthy causes and charitable organizations.

He and his wife live in Colorado, and they are the parents of college-age children. Over the years, Doug has spent much of his time as a classroom volunteer, a youth basketball coach, an advocate for local environmental issues, a frequent traveler, and a craftsman, building a cabin in the Rocky Mountains.

THE ART OF WEALTH

THE ART
OF
WEALTH

Strategies for Success

Translated from the Sanskrit,
with Commentary, by

THOMAS CLEARY

Health Communications, Inc.
Deerfield Beach, Florida

www.hci-online.com

Library of Congress Cataloging-in-Publication Data

Kauṭalya.
   [Selections. English. 1998]
   The art of wealth : strategies for success / [Kauṭalya] ; translated from the
Sanskrit, with commentary, by Thomas Cleary.
     p. cm.
   Includes bibliographical references and index.
   ISBN 1-55874-541-6 (trade pbk.)
   1. Success. 2. Wealth. I. Cleary, Thomas F., date. II. Title.
BJ1611.2.K3813 1998
332.024'01—dc21   97-43796
                                                       CIP

Publisher: Health Communications, Inc.
               3201 S.W. 15th Street
               Deerfield Beach, Florida 33442-8190

INTRODUCTION

Those who have not acquired wealth in youth
ruminate like old herons on a pond with no fish.

—*Gautama Buddha*

Money talks, even in hell.

—*Japanese proverb*

More than two thousand years ago, a mysterious Indian philosopher formulated a science of wealth and sovereignty, synthesizing social, psychological, economic, and strategic principles into a comprehensive program.

Immortalizing this science in the Sanskrit language, an elegant compound of poetry and logic, the philosopher taught his methods to an obscure herdsman-soldier. Following the philosopher's advice, the herdsman-soldier rose in the world and ultimately succeeded in founding the greatest Indian empire in history.

The herdsman-turned-emperor was Chandragupta Maurya, founder of the empire and dynasty named after him. Because he rose from obscurity, it is not known when he was born. Referred to by the Greeks as Sandracottus, Chandragupta flourished in the last quarter of the fourth century B.C.E.

Uniting most of the Indian subcontinent for the first time under one rule, Chandragupta went on to incorporate much of Kashmir and Afghanistan, driving invading Greeks in Alexander's wake back as far as Persia.

The Maurya dynasty ruled for nearly one and a half centuries, from about 325 to 182 B.C.E. Emperor Ashoka, grandson of the founder, who extended the empire by conquest and reigned from about 273 to 232 B.C.E., is particularly famous among the later Maurya rulers.

Eventually converting to Buddhism and renouncing warfare, Emperor Ashoka became a distinguished patron of culture. He convened a historic Buddhist council and established an international Buddhist mission spreading the wisdom of Buddha through the Indian subcontinent and west to Afghanistan, Persia, Greece, Egypt and beyond. The Edicts of Ashoka, pious exhortations inscribed on stone pillars throughout the empire, are one of the great monuments of the old world.

Through the Maurya conquests and cultural missions, Indo-Aryan civilization absorbed ancient Indian cultures on an unprecedented scale, and brought renewed contact with other branches of Aryan civilization—Greek, Latin and Celtic—each of which had in the meantime absorbed elements of numerous other ancient cultures in the course of migration and settlement in various regions.

While the ancient profusion of abstract philosophies makes the very idea of Indian thought seem exotic and rarefied to many people today, the fact is that nothing could be more concrete and practical than what we find in the classical Sanskrit *Art of Wealth*. Nevertheless, it cannot be considered a purely materialistic way of thought by any means because it is intimately connected with the psychological and moral condition of the individual and society.

Kauthilya, the thinker whose philosophy of wealth and sovereignty inspired and informed the remarkable success of the Maurya empire, has been called the Aristotle of India and the Machiavelli of India.

Because he integrates a broad spectrum of human concerns into his thinking, pursuing ethical principles with strategic sciences, Kauthilya's ideas naturally resemble other classical practical philosophies of both East and West. Some of the obvious parallels are illustrated here, to enrich the appreciation of Kauthilya's thought.

Common sense and ancient traditions both tell us that no formula for success in any domain can work like a magic charm, as it were, by mechanical application irrespective of the times, the circumstances and the people concerned. Perhaps the most interesting, creative and productive modern-day use of the perennial classics of great civilizations may be realized through the stimulus to thinking that the classics can provide when they are used freely and without bigotry or bias; employed for exercise rather than indoctrination; and considered rationally and reflectively rather than religiously and dogmatically.

THE ART
OF
WEALTH

The root of happiness is justice;
the root of justice is wealth.
The root of wealth is sovereignty;
the root of sovereignty is mastery of the faculties.

The root of happiness is justice because we can hardly be happy if we are constantly in conflict, constantly on guard, constantly worried, constantly scheming.

If we are so inconsiderate or so selfish that we habitually offend others and even transgress on their rights, we cannot possibly live a happy life, simply because of the friction and antagonism unjust behavior creates.

It is not possible to lead a happy life, moreover, if there is no sense of order or justice on which individuals and communities may draw in their dealings with one another, simply because of the insecurity and suspicion such conditions of mistrust will breed.

The root of justice is wealth because in conditions of overpowering want and need, instinct overpowers intelligence. Mencius, a Chinese sage who lived about the same era as the Indian philosopher Kauthilya, remarked that in his time fire and water were so plentiful that anyone would give them when asked; if only beans and wheat were that plentiful, the sage mused, no one would not be benevolent.

There is also another reason why justice is rooted in wealth. "Poverty gags the intelligent man," says the Sufi sage Hadrat Ali, "preventing him from making his case, and the pauper is a stranger in his own town." People who are not successful in the terms understood by their own societies are not respected, making it hard for them to obtain justice from the social system. Being unable to protect themselves, they are therefore unable to protect others. In this sense, a reasonable degree of affluence is a necessary accomplishment for anyone who bears social responsibility, especially responsibility for others.

It is a matter of daily experience, nevertheless, that material wealth alone is not all that is required for security and justice. Surely there are wealthy people who are still unsatisfied, ambitious and predatory. This is why, in the traditional Aryan social system, moral education precedes professional commitment.

The Sufi sage Hadrat Ali said, "There is no wealth like intelligence, and no poverty like ignorance." The intelligent one without material wealth may gain the materially necessary by application of that intelligence, while the wealthy one without intelligence is likely to lose existing advantages by failing to apply intelligence to his appreciation and employment.

So the root of wealth is not wealth itself, but that whereby wealth may be honestly secured and justly employed. The pundit says, therefore, that the root of wealth is sovereignty. This means more than a sphere of influence; it means the capacity to apply oneself and utilize one's resources autonomously, according to the dictates of intelligence, as best suited to the pursuit of well-being, justice and happiness.

Sovereignty begins with the self, with self-mastery, this sovereignty extending to the social and material environment in proportion to the inner development of the human faculties. Therefore the root of sovereignty, says the pundit, is control of the faculties. This has a two-fold meaning: self-control and self-application.

Mastery of the faculties as self-control is the root of sovereignty in that it enables the individual to work in the world with a buoyant heart, not subject to deviation by temporary attractions or diversions. The ancient Chinese strategists spoke of using desire and anger to manipulate opponents; those who have mastered their own faculties are to that degree winners, in that they cannot be ruined by such tactics.

Mastery of the faculties as self-application is also at the root of sovereignty, in that inner potential is useless unless it is mobilized. This mobilization of inner potential must correspond in some way, furthermore, to an existing outer potential. The ability to perceive, apprehend, and effectively employ this correspondence of possibility and opportunity, moreover, is also an integral part of self-mastery, or mastery of the faculties.

From mastery of the senses, sovereignty; from sovereignty, wealth; from wealth, justice; and from justice, happiness—this, in sum, is the outline of the whole art and science of wealth. The aphorisms proceed from here, elucidating the process of moral and intellectual development through which one realizes self-mastery, sovereignty, wealth, justice and happiness.

The root of mastery of the faculties is guidance;
the root of guidance is attendance upon elders.
From attendance upon elders comes discernment;
by means of discernment one may prosper.

The root of mastery of the faculties is guidance because it is impossible to attain control of one's faculties in an arbitrary manner. Not only is this impossible; moreover, the attempt is dangerous. Popularized versions of Eastern teachings sometimes suggest that mastery of the faculties can be attained just by some sort of meditation, concentration or yogic practice, but the well-documented fact is that oversimplified mental disciplines practiced in isolation for personalistic motives actually trigger psychological disturbances, harden fixations, and foster delusional thought and behavior.

No one could fairly deny that a certain degree of discipline and cultivation is necessary for life in the world, in the midst of society, where one is dealing with other people day in and day out. The inner life also can be cultivated, with beneficial effects on the outer life; but biased concentration on one facet of our being will inevitably produce an imbalanced or incomplete development.

Both the inner and outer life, as well as their interaction and interrelation in experience, respond adaptively to guidance in the process of their unfolding and their evolution. In the absence of conscious cultivation, that guidance may be no more than a series of more or less random impacts caused by happenstance and conditioned by historical and environmental accidents. The result is a personality without inner coherence, an individual without intrinsic autonomy. This is not a moral judgment so much as a description of bound energy.

The countermeasure to willy-nilly personal development is "attendance upon elders," or listening receptively to the voice of experience. As Ali, the Sufi sage, remarks, "There is no backup like consultation." Buddha said, "Just as the tongue discerns the taste of the soup, the intelligent one will realize the truth right away by associating with the wise for even a while." A Chan classic says, "Association with the good is like walking through dew and mist—although they do not soak you, in time your clothes become moist." Buddha said, "For those who are always courteous and respectful of elders, four things increase: life, beauty, happiness and strength."

The voice of experience comes to us in different forms. Sometimes the "elders" from whose company we gain discernment are experienced and knowledgeable people in our families, neighborhoods, and places of work and recreation. Sometimes the "elders" are words of wisdom from our sacred traditions, our scriptures, our classics, our histories, our stories, our music, our art. Sometimes the "elders" are rocks, trees, rivers, hills and other features of nature, teaching us the lessons of their experiences and the natural laws of causality they must obey. As a Chinese thinker wrote, "Learning is an everyday affair, in which awareness should be exercised in each situation."

Discernment thus developed through observation, experience and actual practice becomes a permanent part of the personality, a permanent asset, a form of abstract wealth that can generate concrete prosperity by application to the potential of the times and circumstances in which one finds oneself. "That deed is well done," said Buddha, "that is not followed by regret, whose consequences are attended by joy and happiness." This appropriateness of action, the foundation of success, can be realized through the attainment and exercise of authentic discernment, seeing and knowing things as they have been, currently are and possibly can be.

⫘⫘⫘

The successful individual realizes self-mastery; one with self-mastery enjoys all riches.

Self-mastery enables the successful individual to enjoy all riches in a number of ways. To begin with, self-mastery underpins the patience and diligence needed to create wealth. In the process, self-mastery enables one to avoid being deviated from long-term goals by the seduction of short-term gains.

When success has been attained, furthermore, self-mastery prevents the successful individual from becoming complacent and squandering the fruits of honest effort.

There are many traditional expressions that address this issue. A Buddhist proverb says, "The spoils of war are used up in celebration." If we only labor to consume, and only consume whatever we earn, there is no further progress. The question of how we use the fruits of our labors beyond fulfilling the needs of our dependents is crucial to the perpetuation and progress of prosperity.

It might seem that nothing tries our souls like failure and defeat, but setbacks can actually stimulate determination and improvement. When we win some success, however, we are tempted to feel self-satisfied, and this can make us stagnate, or fill our heads with inflated ideas of our worth. Thus Ali said, "There is no test like fulfillment." So it is the one with self-mastery who can really enjoy all riches.

Attainment of wealth creates prosperity for the people;
by virtue of the people's prosperity,
even a leaderless domain will be orderly.

The ancient Chinese classic *I Ching* says, "Those above secure their homes by kindness to those below." One of the greatest enjoyments of wealth is in its sharing. Just as the successful individual who loses self-mastery squanders the wealth so painstakingly created, however, sharing wealth with squanderers achieves the same effect, with even greater rapidity. The generation and employment of wealth to create an ever widening circle of prosperity, in contrast, eliminates the consumptive effects of senseless consumption.

If people reasonably and conscientiously pursue occupations that generate wealth for themselves and others, the social fabric can be basically maintained by the shared sense of common interest, or the common sense of shared interest, the pragmatic perception that the good of individuals and the good of the community are inextricably intertwined.

Seen from this point of view, religious commandments like "Love your neighbor as yourself" do not appear to be heroic ideals of self-abnegation, but practical appreciations of the fact that our neighbors are indeed a part of ourselves; our very subsistence, to say nothing of our happiness, depends in many ways upon our neighbors in the widest sense of this word.

The emergence of social order from mutual recognition as part of one another is a natural process, calling into play the reason and goodwill of all who consciously participate. When the activity of an individual, or of a coordinated body of individuals, generates wealth beyond immediate needs, the total profit does not consist solely of the wealth itself, but also of the creative redeployment of excess wealth, of the development of creative wealth. Whether in the life of the individual, of a family, of a corporation or of a nation, the function of wealth in the well-being of the whole body will ultimately determine the future state of the organization.

The wrath of the populace is the most serious anger of all.

The wrath of the populace is most serious because it undermines solidarity and cooperation, and, furthermore, displaces energy from constructive and creative activities to defensive or remedial measures. Whether in government, business or even social life, the opposition of rivals or enemies cannot compare with that of one's own people. Not only does internal disruption compromise the organism from within, it also creates increased vulnerability to pressures or threats from outside.

This idea is well represented in other traditions. The classical Chinese philosopher Mencius said that the basis of the state is not the government but the people. Confucius said that loss of trust is worse than death because "there has always been death, but without trust it is impossible to stand." Similarly, when the prophet Muhammad appointed a governor to Yemen, he warned him to "Beware the cry of the oppressed, for there is no screen between it and God."

The ancient *I Ching,* one of the major sourcebooks of both Confucian and Taoist tradition, also speaks to this point: "Cultivated people distribute blessings to reach those below them, while avoiding presumption of virtue." Huanchu, Taoist thinker of the Ming dynasty, wrote, "If people who are lucky enough to obtain official positions and be well fed and housed do not make it their concern to establish good education and do good works, even if they live a hundred years it is as if they had never lived at all."

Responsibility toward society is considered normal in classical traditions, not only in view of the social nature of humankind and the need for cooperative order to secure material subsistence, but also in the sense of gratitude and appreciation for the amenities and comforts made possible by the collaboration of a multitude of individuals and many walks of life in a coherent and mutually satisfactory social structure.

It is better to have no master than to have an unruly master.

It is better to have no commitments than to be committed to an arbitrary and erratic authority. Gautama Buddha said, "One who walks with fools will sorrow a long way." He also said, "It is better to walk alone;

there is no companionship with a fool. Walk alone, like an elephant in the forest." The more dedicated the effort, the more concentrated the mind, the more critical the question of whether or not the dedication and concentration are rightly directed.

The Sung dynasty Confucian sage Cheng Yi, writing on the subject of following leaders rightly and wrongly, defined "following downward" as "following those in error, abandoning understanding and pursuing ignorance." Speaking of true leadership, the *I Ching* says, "Leaders draw on limitless resources of education and thought to embrace and protect the people without bound." When there is no authentic leadership, however, the same classic says, "Cultivated people can stand alone without fear."

Having prepared oneself, one should seek accompanied; one without allies has no certainty of counsel.

These are the three basic requirements of effectiveness: self-preparation, sound advice and deliberate effort.

"Having prepared oneself" means that nothing can be done without having first prepared oneself. In *The Art of War,* Sun Tzu says that successful warriors are those who secure victory first, and only then go into battle.

"One should seek accompanied" means that the knowledge, views and ideas of others are an important resource in pursuing a constructive endeavor. Confucius said he could find teachers anywhere, by objective observation, taking to the good and avoiding the bad. The *I Ching* says, "Cultivated people form associations for discussion and action."

A single wheel does not make it possible to move around.

Human beings are social creatures by nature, not only in the context of our emotional and intellectual drives, but also in the context of our productive and creative drives. Even when people are solitary and alone, they are nonetheless still part of a totality without which nothing could be alive.

Privacy and companionship in due proportion, solitude and society in appropriate measure, are equally necessary to individual health and integrity, as the full significance of the integral individual unfolds itself and inspires others in the midst of a rich and complex environment embracing many levels of experience in both mental and material dimensions.

An ally is one who is the same in happiness and misery.

Someone who cleaves to you in good times but vanishes in hard times is not really an ally, for hard times are when allies are needed most. Someone who is glad to share your gains but unwilling to share your losses is not much of a partner, as those who stand only to gain and have nothing to lose are missing half of normal motivation.

A Chan Buddhist proverb says, "My parents were the ones who gave birth to me; my companions were the ones who raised me." The issue of human associations has perennially been considered fundamental because it is in the nature of human beings to transmit impulses and attitudes simply through association. It was originally for this reason, more than for reasons of social or economic status, that knowledge was once most commonly concentrated and passed on in families, since the family was a natural center of human association.

The Sufi sage Ali counseled his own son on the subject of allies in these terms: "Do not befriend a fool, for he hurts you when he wants to help you. And do not befriend a stingy man, for he will distance himself from you when he is most needed." The *I Ching* says, "Cultivated people stand without changing places." Gautama Buddha said, "The sight of the noble is good, association with them is always happy. One who never sees fools will be happy forever."

—

The thinking individual should designate an adviser who is a fitting counterpart to oneself.

It might seem reasonable to choose someone quite different from yourself as an adviser, on the premise that this will provide you with different perspectives and different points of view. Advice that comes from a level of knowledge or a history of experience that is very different, however, may for that very reason prove to be impractical for the individual concerned.

For advice to be practical, it must be within the range of possibility. However good advice may be, if it is beyond one's ability to implement that advice, it is not really useful. Therefore an adviser needs to really understand an advisee well in order to provide advice that is sound in conception and practical in action. That is why it is recommended that one choose an adviser who is like oneself. The Taoist strategist Master of Demon Valley said, "Those with the same voice call to each other." Confucius said, "Those whose paths are not the same do not consult one another."

One who is unruly should not be made an adviser simply out of affection.

Personal feelings can distort our perceptions of others' character and cause us to misunderstand what they are communicating to us. We may like certain people, feel affection toward them and enjoy their company, but that does not mean that these are the people to whom we should turn for advice. The choice of advisers has to be more objective than subjective, as Confucius suggests: "See what they do, observe the how and the why, and examine their basic premises."

A Chan Buddhist dictum states that it is wise to see what is good about what one dislikes and to see what is bad about what one likes; the same is certainly true of people, whether acquaintances or strangers. When we understand the shortcomings and flaws of those toward whom we feel affection, and also can see the strengths and virtues of those whom we may not personally like, this balance makes it possible to work with people harmoniously under any conditions.

There is also an important principle to be observed here from the point of view of the adviser. When Confucius was asked how to work for a ruler, he said, "Don't deceive him, even if you have to offend him." Human feelings being what they are, just as personal affections might induce someone to choose the wrong adviser, personal affections might also inhibit a chosen adviser from giving the right advice for fear of causing emotional upset. As a Chan proverb says, "Sincere words may offend the ear."

In everyday life, we are ordinarily influenced by what we see and hear, even when (and sometimes especially when) we do not consciously register that influence. The sources of this influence naturally include the people around us, so to some degree we are more or less constantly exposed to the suggestions emanating from the social environment.

This is why classic traditions make so much of human associations in education and development. Buddha said, "If you find a prudent companion, a wise associate who leads a good life, having overcome all troubles, travel with that one, uplifted and aware."

One who is learned
and innocent of pretense
should be made a counselor.

It may go without saying that a counselor should be knowledgeable, but the fact of human psychology is that pride tends to go along with attainment, even to the point where it can be exaggerated into pretense, which then can outstrip reality. Ali said, "Many an intellectual has been killed by his ignorance, the knowledge he had with him failing to profit him."

This point is emphasized by many ancient sages. Confucius said, "Even if you have fine abilities, if you are arrogant and stingy, the rest is not worth considering." Huanchu said, "Those who make a show of morality are inevitably slandered on moral grounds; those who make a show of learning are always blamed on account of learning." Lao-tzu said, "To know unconsciously is best; to presume to know what you don't is sick. Only by recognizing the sickness of sickness is it possible not to be sick." The Taoist Master of the Hidden Storehouse said, "Those who are worthy of the name 'wise' do not call themselves wise."

All undertakings begin with counsel.

The master strategist Sun Tzu wrote, "Assess the advantages in taking advice, then structure your forces accordingly." A Chan proverb says, "Strategy at headquarters determines success abroad." Expending energy without direction drains people and renders them ineffective in the long run. The Taoist sage Lao-tzu said, "The journey of ten thousand miles begins with the first step." Without prudent planning, which includes seeking and taking advice from reliable and worthy sources, there is little chance of taking the first step in the right direction. As another Chan proverb says, "The crooked does not hide the straight." According to natural law, the result of an activity must be in conformity with the cause and conditions of its pursuit.

Misguided effort takes us further afield the harder we try. Diligence cannot compensate for misdirection. This is why counsel or guidance naturally includes a realistic assessment of one's situation and abilities. The Master of the Hidden Storehouse said, "The effectiveness of a mirror in showing a leader what he looks like is small compared to the effectiveness of educated people in showing a leader what he is like." The

Master of Demon Valley said, "There is nothing to do but value wisdom. Wisdom employs what is unknown to most people, and can use what is invisible to most people. Once wisdom is in use, one acts on one's own by seeing what can be chosen and working on it; one acts for others by seeing what is unavoidable and working on that."

Fulfillment of what is to be done
lies in keeping security of counsel;
one who divulges advice ruins the task.

Keeping security of counsel protects plans from the interference of the interloper who aims to take advantage of others, from the attack of the spoiler who seeks the downfall of the able, from the impatience of the overeager one who seeks to profit right away and from the confusion of the controversialist who wants to argue and get his way.

There is, furthermore, also the logic of silence as space in which to act or maneuver. A master plan spoken too soon might become excessively rigidified in the minds of hearers, to the point where necessary flexibility could be lost. Strategic thinker Mei Yaochen wrote, "Insofar as you adapt and adjust accordingly in the face of opposition, how could you say what you are going to do beforehand?"

Through carelessness one will come under
the control of enemies:
counsel is to be kept guarded from all doors.

Inscrutability and impassivity, often thought to be character traits of certain peoples, are ordinarily results of training in the practice of reserve. Reserve, or discretion, is deliberately cultivated for the simple reason, articulated so concisely here by our pundit, that carelessness causes vulnerability. Those who misunderstand the nature of the strategy and take the products and effects of this training too personally inevitably lose out in both affective and competitive interaction with others.

When their brains can be easily picked and their inner thoughts revealed, or their emotions easily triggered and their private sensitivities exposed, people can be readily manipulated by those who seek to turn the frailties of the human condition to their own personal advantage. The Taoist Huainan Masters said, "When like and dislike began to have their says, order and chaos went their ways."

This principle is, quite naturally, emphasized very strongly in strategic literature. The Master of Demon Valley said, "In the use of tactical strategies, it is better to be private than public; and alliance is even better than mere privacy, alliance meaning a partnership that has no gaps."

It is in the state of "having no gaps" that the integrity of an individual, a relationship or a group is maintained. It is in this sense, more than in the sense of sinister secrecy, that the Master of Demon Valley said, "The Way of mastery is in concealment and covertness." Lao-tzu explains, "Is it empty talk, the old saying that tact keeps you whole? When truthfulness is complete, it still resorts to this."

By fulfillment of counsel, dominion grows;
they say keeping counsel secret
is of utmost importance.

Mastery develops through putting good advice into practice. Fulfillment of counsel demands first of all that one recognize what good advice is, how feasible it is, how valuable it is and what is necessary to its execution.

These preliminary discernments may be elementary, but they are not necessarily easy. Not only must one develop one's own perceptions, one must also cultivate the right company.

According to a Chinese Buddhist master of the Sung dynasty, writing at a time when religion and culture seemed to be flourishing, "It is hard to find anyone who will say that what is right is right and what is wrong is wrong, who is balanced, true and upright, free from hypocrisy."

Keeping counsel secret, or confidential, is not only important as a normal security measure; it is also important at an even earlier stage of planning, the stage of assessment of advice. Silently keeping one's peace while in the process of hearing counsel and evaluating it reduces random interference and fosters cool consideration.

The dual function of secrecy, for security and for privacy, is captured perfectly by the Taoist Master of Demon Valley, who explains that internal secrecy maintains the integrity of the group, while external secrecy maintains the integrity of the operation: "Those who are themselves on the inside but speak to outsiders are ostracized; those who are themselves outsiders but whose talk goes too deep are in danger."

Pursuing this line of thought, it can be seen how tactful reserve can enable one to avoid frustration by hostility and contention. The Master of Demon Valley said, "What people do not like should not be forced on them; what does not concern people should not be taught to them." Thus eventual success may be furthered by keeping things confidential until the one who is ultimately responsible has determined the needs and capacities, the mentalities and concerns, of those likely to be affected by a course of action.

Counsel is a lamp to one in the dark about what is to be done.

It is better to do nothing than to act at random and do something wrong. The advantage of gaining other perspectives may be there, but the fact remains that when one does not know what to do oneself, one will not necessarily recognize sound counsel simply by its presence. When in the dark, it is not enough just to follow direction; in order to tell whether it is worth following, one needs some sense of where this direction is to lead.

Following advice blindly when in the dark is to go from darkness to darkness. Authentic counsel, therefore, includes within it means of testing its probity. Proven character, intelligence and knowledge on the part of the person, perceptible logic, reason, and contextual feasibility in the advice—when these are all there, then counsel is a "lamp to one in the darkness" because it does not simply beckon enthusiasm or trust; it removes the darkness itself.

The faults of others are seen
through the eyes of advisers;
when advice is given, let there be no hostility.

Personal feelings or private debts of some kind may blind one to the shortcomings of associates in professional life. In such cases, the observations of objective advisers are of inestimable value, considering the loss and injury that can result from keeping the wrong company.

As long as emotional or other biases have indeed compromised one's ability to see people as they really are, one is not likely to be receptive to other points of view. According to a story in a Buddhist scripture, when a king once consulted a sage about which of his sons to designate as heir to the throne, the sage replied with withering criticisms of each and every one of the princes. This so enraged the king that he wanted to have the sage put to death. Now the sage laughingly bade the king to spare his life, for by such candor with a king had he not proven himself a fool, no sage at all, unworthy of a hearing?

While tact is surely needed in advisers, there is a limit to which truth can be covered without compromise. What is also needed is receptivity in those who seek counsel on account of the responsibilities of their positions. One who is impatient with anything but his own opinions has a hard time learning, even from experience.

People in positions of power have a correspondingly powerful need for the clarity to see beyond private feelings and evaluate others objectively. Yagyu Munenori, tutor to a shogun of seventeenth-century Japan, makes this point with great urgency in the context of political organization: "There are only a few people close to a ruler, perhaps five or ten. The majority of people are remote from rulers. When many people resent their ruler, they will express their feelings. When those who are close to the ruler have been after their own private interests all along, not acting in consideration of the leadership, they serve in such a way that the populace resents the ruler. Then when a crisis occurs, these very ones who are close to the ruler will be the first to set upon him!"

If one is not receptive to information or advice that would make it possible to see hidden treachery before it surfaces, there will always be pitfalls that remain imperceptible. Yagyu wrote, "If you do not see the dynamic of a situation, you may remain too long in company where you should not be, and get into trouble for no reason."

In *Forest of Wisdom,* a Chinese collection of Sung dynasty Chan extracts, it is explained that the best way to learn to take good advice is to learn how to recognize sincere advisers. As one thinker says, "Retain those who are more mature, and keep away opportunistic flatterers. The value in this is that there will be no slander of corruption, and no fac- tionalist disruption."

Opportunistic flatterers may be the very ones to strangle off avenues of sincere advice, and their interference may in fact be perversely wel- comed by those who secretly wish to be relieved of responsibility for hard choices and difficult decisions. In any case, however, those who get the reputation of listening to opportunistic flatterers will be abandoned by the intelligent, and mired in the disputes and machinations of self- seeking "courtiers" vying for attention and influence.

Assent is when there is unanimity of three.

Two people may fool or flatter each other into believing themselves to be correct and then enjoy the illusion too much to pay any attention to another opinion. It is harder for a group of three (or more) to reach any sort of facile, uncritical unanimity, so as a result more questioning, thought and reflection go on before a decision or a determination is reached. Thus the process of advice and consent has a reduced margin of error.

This phenomenon is reflected in a popular Japanese proverb that says, "Three people together have the wisdom of a sage." The nature of everyday reality, moreover, is that of agreement, or convention, as illustrated by the Chinese proverb that says, "If three people call it a turtle, then it's a turtle." When there is "unanimity of three," this means that there is a practical agreement, a working convention, which can be used as a basis of coordinated undertakings and cooperative endeavors.

Advisers are those who see the true reason for what is to be done and what is not to be done.

An aim may be deemed desirable, and a plan conceived for its attainment, yet the enthusiasm and endeavor may turn out to be futile if the aim is unrealistic, the plan is unfeasible or perception of relevant conditions is unclear. The fact remains, however, that when desire produces enthusiasm and enthusiasm spawns effort, cold practicalities may be overlooked in the heat of the moment of inspiration.

Therefore consideration of reason and means is as important as generation of ideas and aspirations. When we truly understand why we are doing one thing or avoiding another, then we can reach the peak of effectiveness. If we only know where we want to go but not how to get there, agitation to get going may delude us into thinking we will find our way as we go along.

Authentic advice, then, does not simply say what to do and what not to do, but makes this clear in the process of explaining why and why not. When causes and effects are understood, advice can be recognized without doubt and applied without distortion. The Master of Demon Valley said, "Strategic planning is the pivot of survival and destruction. If thinking is not fitting, then hearing is unclear and timing is inaccurate, resulting in mistakes in planning. Then intention is unreliable, vacuous and insubstantial."

Advice is betrayed by six ears.

Six ears means three people. There is an ancient Chinese saying that "Six ears do not have the same plans," meaning that it is difficult to maintain security when secrets are shared. The image is made more graphic by the use of the expression "six ears" instead of "three people" insofar as it alludes to "two ears" per person, suggesting that the mind of an individual may also be divided within itself. One ear may be hearing one thing, as it were, while the other ear hears another; one ear may be tuned to a private conference while the other ear may be receiving outside signals. The resulting complexity of differences in views, sources and interpretations then complicates the problem of security.

One whose affection remains sure in adversities is a friend.

It may go without saying that a "fair-weather friend," one who disappears in hard times, is in reality no friend at all, but there is neither wisdom nor consolation in realizing the truth after the fact. The Sufi sage Hadrat Ali counseled his son, "Do not befriend a stingy man, for he will distance himself from you when he is most needed; and do not befriend a profligate, as he will sell you for a trifle."

Although it is therefore desirable to recognize reality and falsehood in people before having anything to do with them, still one can hardly be comfortable in society if one is habitually suspicious and distrusting.

The appropriate balance is not necessarily easy to attain, particularly in a highly competitive society. Confucius said, "They are wise who do not anticipate deception and do not consider dishonesty, yet are aware of them from the start." This degree of serene clarity takes a lifetime of cultivation.

When there is more than individual responsibility involved in personal associations, when the total complex of official, professional, and social rights and duties is influenced by the company one keeps, after-the-fact recognition of fair-weather friends may be disastrous. For this reason, ways of testing people have been developed over the ages by practical thinkers in political, military, religious and professional fields.

Questionnaires and written tests do not necessarily do the job quite thoroughly enough. "The difficulty of knowing people troubles even sages," said a famous Chan Buddhist teacher of Sung dynasty China, explaining that "You cannot know their behavior for sure just from one answer or one question. Indeed, clever talkers cannot always be trusted in fact, while clumsy talkers may have irrefutable reason."

Strategists writing for political and military leaders have considered this issue one of crucial importance. The great Chinese leader K'ung Ming, whose exploits are immortalized in *The Romance of the Three Kingdoms,* wrote in his manual *The Way of the General*: "Hard though it be to know people, there are ways. First is to question them concerning right and wrong, to observe their ideas. Second is to exhaust all their arguments, to see how they change. Third is to consult with them about strategy, to see how perceptive they are. Fourth is to announce that there is trouble, to see how brave they are. Fifth is to get them intoxicated, to observe their inner nature. Sixth is to present them with the prospect of gain, to see how modest they are. Seventh is to give them a task to do within a specific time, to see how trustworthy they are."

The severity of the methods employed naturally depends on the nature of the situation, especially on the margin for error. The Greek philosopher Plato believed that the essence of whatever method used to evaluate people was to see whether they had greater taste for truth than for material comfort; he said, "You should test someone who resorts to you by deprivation and unjust treatment. If one patiently endures the deprivation but complains about the unjust treatment, you may attach him to yourself and treat him well. If one patiently endures unjust treatment and complains about deprivation, however, you may leave him and avoid him."

Power is attained by winning friends.
The powerful one strives to gain what is lacking.
Gaining what is lacking is not for the lazy.
The lazy one, moreover, cannot keep
even what he has gotten.

What is in the keeping of the lazy one, furthermore,
does not grow; he does not direct employees.
Gaining what has not been gained,
maintaining it, developing it and employing it:
these four are the essentials of sovereignty.

Cooperation, focus, determination and effort are all elements of attaining success. Attentiveness and diligence in consolidating gains and fostering growth, employing the fruits of success effectively, are all elements of maintaining success.

The Master of Demon Valley said, "Solidifying intent refers to formulation of mental energy into thought. The mind should be calm and quiet, thought should be deep and far-reaching. When the mind is calm and quiet, then brilliant measures are conceived; when thought is deep and far-reaching, then strategic plans are perfected. When brilliant measures are conceived, then the will cannot be disturbed. When strategic plans are perfected, then achievements cannot be blocked."

The course of practical philosophy
depends on the essentials of sovereignty;
system and arrangement are based
on the essentials of sovereignty.

The Master of Demon Valley said, "Human leaders have a natural pivot, producing, growing, harvesting and storing, which is not to be opposed; those who oppose it inevitably decline, even if they flourish. This way of nature is the overall guideline for human leaders."

The system is dependent upon
application in one's own sphere.
Preparedness is focused
on neighboring territories;
neighboring territories are a source
of alliance and discord.

To be successful, it is necessary to mind one's own business and do one's own task, but to enhance and to safeguard success, it is also necessary to consider what others are doing. It may be possible to make alliances, and it may be imperative to establish defenses. However one has mastered one's own sphere of action, it is not possible to control others as oneself; therefore it is essential to understand others, and know whether they are likely sources of discord or suitable partners in alliance

The Art of War says, "In ancient times, skillful warriors first made themselves invincible, and then watched for vulnerability in their opponents."

One who follows practical philosophy is sovereign.

Random action based upon the enthusiasm or ambition of the moment is not a secure path. A rational, intelligent, systematic approach to practical organization and tactical strategy enhances chances of success. The Master of Demon Valley said, "Without wisdom and knowledge, you cannot preserve your home with justice and cannot preserve your country with the Way."

An immediately neighboring population is a rival;
one that is separated by an intermediate territory
is a friend.
Rivalry and friendship will be as such for a reason.

The Master of Demon Valley said, "If there is outward friendliness but inward estrangement, reconcile the inner relationship. If there is inward friendliness but outward estrangement, reconcile the outward relationship."

One who is in decline should make alliances.
Power is the reason for uniting,
for those who seek it.
Metal does not unite with metal
without being heated.

The Master of Demon Valley said, "The method of opposition and alliance demands that you gauge your own ability and intelligence, and assess your own strengths and weaknesses, seeing who does not compare among those far and near. Only then can you advance and withdraw freely and independently."

The strong should fight with the weak,
not with a superior or an equal.
Contention with the powerful
is like battle with elephants;
an unfired vessel is destroyed
by collision with another unbaked one.

The Art of War says, "In ancient times, those known as good warriors prevailed when it was easy to prevail. Therefore the victories of good warriors are not noted for cleverness or bravery. So their victories in battle are not flukes. Their victories are not flukes because they position themselves where they will surely win, prevailing over those who have already lost. So it is that good warriors take their stand on ground where they cannot lose, and do not overlook conditions that make an opponent prone to defeat."

The action of enemies should be watched.
Alliance is to be made on an individual basis.
One should maintain one's own security
from the wrath of the unfriendly.

The Master of Demon Valley said, "Those in ancient times who skillfully operated countries always measured the powers in the land and figured out the psychological conditions of local leaders. If measurement of powers is not thorough, you do not know the strong and the weak, the light and the heavy. If psychological conditions are not figured out thoroughly, you do not know the activities of hidden changes and developments."

Those of lesser capability must depend
on the powerful.
Reliance on the powerless brings misery.
Let one go to a ruler as to a fire;
one should not act in opposition to the ruler.

The Master of Demon Valley said, "In the relationship between ruler and minister, or between superior and subordinate, there may be those who are on friendly terms in spite of distance, and there may be those who are alienated in spite of closeness."

One should not wear exaggerated clothing.
One should not act as if one of the gods.
Double-dealing is done
when there are two envious parties.

The Taoist Master of the Hidden Storehouse said, "When a country is going to perish, the officials at court are splendidly attired, their countenances are harmonious, their speech is flowery and genteel, their movements are careful and elegant. Although the administration of a moribund country may outwardly appear to be harmonious and obedient, inwardly the officials harbor suspicions and aversions, each pursuing his own personal aims, secretly plotting each other harm."

One who is extreme in addiction to some passion
does not achieve what is to be done.
Even with elephants, chariots, cavalry and infantry,
someone controlled by the senses will perish.

The Master of the Hidden Storehouse said, "When fashions fan the flames of desire, the people are not faithful and pure; they are ashamed of simplicity and value ostentation."

No task is accomplished
by one devoted to gambling.
Virtue and wealth disappear
from one addicted to hunting.

The *Tao Te Ching* says, "Colors blind people's eyes; sounds deafen their ears; flavors spoil people's palates; the chase and the hunt craze people's minds; goods hard to obtain make people's actions harmful."

Meaningful quest for wealth
is not counted among the vices.
One who is attached to lusts
does not accomplish what is to be done.

The Master of the Hidden Storehouse said, "Things are means of nurturing life, but many deluded people today use their lives to nurture things. Thus they do not know their relative importance. Therefore, in matters of sound, color and flavor, sages take what is beneficial for life and reject what is harmful to life."

Violence of speech is worse
than the burning of fire.

The Master of Demon Valley said, "The defense of insects with shells necessitates thickness and hardness in the shell; the action of poisonous insects necessitates a venomous sting. Thus birds and beasts know how to employ their strengths, while speakers know what is useful and use it."

By harshness in punishment
one becomes odious to all people.

The Master of the Hidden Storehouse said, "The more insistent commands become, the more disorderly people become."

Prosperity abandons one
who is satisfied by material wealth.

The *Tao Te Ching* says, "Which is more, your body or your possessions? Which is more destructive, gain or loss? Extreme fondness means great expense, and abundant possessions mean much loss."

Preparedness for the inimical
is in the science of power.
Practicing the science of power,
one protects the people.

Power leads to success.
Without authority in power,
there is no cabinet of ministers.

The Master of Demon Valley said, "In order to exclude or admit effectively, it is necessary to understand the logic of the Way, figure out coming events and settle any doubts that are sensed. Then there will be no miscalculation in the measures taken, which will then be successful and worthwhile. To direct a populace in productive work is called solidarity and inner cooperation. If the leadership is ignorant and cannot manage, those below get confused without even realizing it. Reverse this by solidarity."

People refrain from what they should not do
on account of punishment.

The Taoist classic *Wen-tzu* says, "The nurturing of life does not force people to do what they cannot do, or stop them from doing what they cannot help doing." *The Way of the General* says, "First organize directives, then organize penalties."

Self-preservation depends on the science of power.
With self-preservation, all becomes secure.
Growth and decay depend on oneself.
Power is to be guided by discernment.

The Master of Demon Valley said, "Focusing the mind's eye is for determining impending perils. Events have natural courses, people have successes and failures. It is imperative to examine movements signaling impending perils."

A ruler is not to be disrespected,
even if weak;
there is no weakness in fire.

The Taoist classic *Chuang-tzu* says, "Don't you know that tiger keepers don't dare to feed them live animals, because of the fury of the tigers killing the prey? And they will not give them whole carcasses either, for the fury of the tigers rending them. By gauging the timing of their hunger and satiety, they guide their furious tempers. Tigers are a different species than humans, but they are nice to their keepers as long as their keepers deal with them according to their nature. Those whom tigers kill are those who deal with them in a manner contrary to their nature."

Action results from power.
Acquisition of wealth is rooted in action.
Justice and pleasure are rooted in wealth.
The root of wealth is work.
Work is accomplished with economy of effort.

Wen-tzu says, "The Way involves respect for what is small and subtle, acting without losing the right timing." The *Tao Te Ching* says, "Plan for difficulty when it is still easy, do the great while it is still small. The most difficult things in the world must be done while they are easy; the greatest things in the world must be done while they are small."

What is approached by expedient means
will not be hard to do.
Without expedient means, work is futile,
even if it is done.
Expedient means are the allies
of those seeking to accomplish something.

Wen-tzu says, "To have many abilities means to be competent in both culture and defense, and to do precisely what is right in terms of your conduct in action and repose, in what you take up and what you put aside, what you dispense with and what you set up."

The aim of work is attained by human effort.
Opportunity goes along with human effort.
Without opportunity, even excessive effort
will be fruitless.

Sufi master Ali said, "The man who gets the worst bargain and is the most unsuccessful in his endeavors is the one who wears out his body in seeking his wealth but is not assisted by destiny toward his aim." He also said, "Waste of an opportunity is torment."

The unfocused cannot act.
Decide first, then set to work.

The Master of Demon Valley said, "The mind's eye is knowledge, focus is practical action."

When a task is ended,
there should be no procrastination
in what's next to be done.

The classic Chinese *I Ching* says, "Ideal people are consistent in their deeds." Sufi master Ali said, "Complacency hinders growth."

The unsteady one
does not accomplish his task.

The *Tao Te Ching* says, "People's works are always spoiled on the verge of completion."

Work goes wrong from disrespect
of what is obtained.

The *Tao Te Ching* says, "The most massive tree grows from a sprout; the highest building rises from a pile of earth; a journey of a thousand miles begins with a step."

Perfectly executed tasks
are hard to find.

The *Tao Te Ching* says, "Be as careful of the end as of the beginning, and nothing will be spoiled."

A task that is an uninterrupted
succession of difficulties
should not be undertaken.

The *I Ching* says, "Coming and going, pitfall upon pitfall. In danger and dependent, one goes into a hole in a pit. Do not act this way."

One who knows the right timing
will get the job done.

Sufi master Ali said, "Stupidity includes hurrying before the right time and waiting until the opportunity has passed."

Through the passage of time,
time itself consumes the results.
In all tasks,
not even a moment of time
is to be wasted.

Sufi master Ali said, "Everyone who is being overtaken by death asks for more time, while everyone who still has time makes excuses for procrastination."

One should begin a task after coming to know
the particulars of the locality and the results.
The expert in practical philosophy
observes the place and time.
Prosperity lasts for one
who acts after observation.
Prosperity forsakes even the fortunate one
who acts without observation.
Observation is to be done by means
of knowledge and inference.

The Master of Demon Valley said, "All strategy has a way, which demands that you find the bases to discover the conditions. . . . People on a treasure hunt use a compass to avoid getting lost: measuring capacities, assessing abilities, and figuring out feelings and psychological conditions are the compass of business and political affairs."

All kinds of success are to be obtained
by all kinds of means.
Let one be devoted
to whatever work one is good at.
One who knows the appropriate means
makes the difficult easy.

Wen-tzu says, "When sages initiate undertakings, they are always based on available resources, which they put to use. Those who are effective in one way are placed in one position; those who have one talent work on one task. When you have the strength for the responsibility, an undertaking is not burdensome; when you have the ability for a task, it is not difficult to perform. Because sages employ them all, people are not abandoned and things are not wasted."

What has been done without knowledge
is not worthy of much esteem.

Even a little bit of well-oriented effort is more productive than a whole lot of disoriented effort.

Even a worm changes forms
for no apparent reason.

People or things that may seem insignificant at one particular point in time are not to be ignored or slighted, for there is no telling what changes the future may bring.

It is the accomplished work
that is to be made known.

The *I Ching* says, "A change is believed on the day of completion." If an undertaking is announced and then fails, the effect on general morale is more negative; if an undertaking is accomplished and then announced, the effect on general morale is more positive.

Even the knowledgeable
have their works go bad
through the detrimental effects
of people or of fate.

Even if the knowledge and talent are there, it is unwise to presume upon success. There may always be interlopers and adversaries, and there is no telling what natural forces, like disasters or sudden changes in conditions, may interfere with an enterprise.

Fate can be restrained
by making peace with it;
humanly caused failure
can be prevented by skill.

The adverse effects of unexpected changes or natural disasters can be minimized by accepting their possibility, preparing for them and coping with them when they happen. The adverse effects of interlopers and adversaries can be minimized by skillful human relations both inside and outside the group.

In failure, the puerile
talk of the obstacles.

When something fails, it is more productive to reflect on what more or what else one could have done than to complain of how hard it was.

One who seeks to accomplish something
must be ruthless;
the calf seeking milk
assails the mother's udder.

Weakness of will is a handicap in an unrelenting world.

Failure at work
comes from lack of effort;
success at work
does not belong to those
who count on luck.

Steady development of skills is more effective and more secure than just getting by from task to task.

The idle one cannot support dependents.

The responsibilities and pleasures of family life, and the development of character their experiences promote, are a lot to lose by laziness.

One who does not see work to be done is blind.

Sufi master Ali said, "Do not ask about what does not exist, for there is work for you in what does exist."

Tasks should be considered
in light of direct evidence,
what is unknown
and inference.

Take into account what can actually be known, what cannot actually be known and what can be figured out.

Prosperity abandons one
who acts without consideration.
One should only begin a task
with knowledge of one's own capacity.

It is common sense to think before acting. This includes considering what kind of information and planning are necessary to make a constructive start. The first thing to assess in structuring an undertaking is the extent of one's own capabilities, so that planning can be realistic and cooperation can be effective.

One who eats the leftovers
after having satisfied his people
is one who consumes ambrosia.

The *I Ching* says, "Good people distribute blessings to reach those below them, while avoiding presumption of virtue."

Avenues of profit increase
through all accomplishments.

Vocations, avocations and hobbies all enrich life in some way. At times an avocation or a hobby may be as profitable as a profession or a vocation. Taking an interest in life and being versatile in one's activities creates an atmosphere of greater enjoyment, a ground of greater potential and also a reservoir of greater resilience in changing times.

The coward does not think
of what is to be done.

Fear of failure is not the same thing as knowing when something is impractical. Fear of failure paralyzes initiative; knowing what makes something practical or impractical concentrates and releases energy.

Let one who seeks work do the job
cognizant of the employer's ways.

One who knows the ways of the cow
gets to enjoy the milk.

The Master of Demon Valley said, "When there is collusion but not solidarity, there is overt alliance but covert alienation."

The self-possessed should not
reveal secrets to the base.

A Japanese proverb says, "The mouth is the door of calamity."

One who is soft by nature is slighted
even by dependents;
the harsh authoritarian
is feared by all.

The essence of Taoist practical philosophy is balancing flexibility and firmness. Flexibility without firmness deteriorates into pliability and weakness; firmness without flexibility hardens into rigidity and oppressiveness.

One should apply discipline as is appropriate.

Reward without merit and punishment without fault undermine the morale of an organization.

The world does not think much
of one with little strength,
even if he is learned.

The world values concrete effect over abstract theory. Someone who has a lot of ideas but never accomplishes anything rarely gains popular respect.

Overburdening depresses a person.

Depression causes people to see things pessimistically, which in turn deepens depression. This undermines initiative, making ordinary tasks themselves seem overburdening, thus propelling the cycle of depression further.

He who announces the fault
of another in company
betrays his own fault.
Self-destructive indeed is the anger
of those who are not self-possessed.

Those who show themselves too ignorant, angry or spiteful to understand the value of compassion and tact in effective criticism will not likely be treated with compassion or tact themselves.

Nothing is unattainable
to those who are truthful.

Confucius said, "Someone who is perfectly sincere can affect things thereby."

Success at work
does not come through recklessness.

Taking risks and taking chances are not the same thing; boldness and recklessness are different states of mind. Gain gotten by chance can also be lost by chance; considering that it may be necessary to take risks sometimes, this must be backed up by basic constancy and deliberate planning.

One who is afflicted by calamity
or suffering pain
forgets it when it is no longer impinging.
There is no continuity when time is wasted.

Realizing that the misery of a trying situation will eventually go away, one can avoid letting distress and downheartedness set the tone of life, and be the more ready to go on without wasting time with depression and regret.

Ruination through risk is better
than ruination without risk.

When you are ruined through risk, you know you took your chances; when you are ruined without risk, you know you were sleeping on your feet. There is less regret in knowing you took your chances than in knowing you were asleep on your feet.

Taking the goods of others in pledge
is purely self-interest.

If there were no self-interest, a loan would be a gift.

Giving is righteous.

There are many different rationales, forms and patterns of giving followed around the world, but there is also something common underlying their diversity. Thus it could be said of every society that "giving," in some form, "is righteous." The structure of the giving recognized as righteous in a particular culture tends to show where the society's heart is.

One who is wealthy but perverse
is not noble, but malicious.

People without conscience might draw great wealth from the produce and labor of a community or society but remain callous to the needs and desires of the people. They might outwardly be considered community leaders in political affairs by virtue of their holdings, and yet be considered bandits by the people and lack the popular support needed to be effective in action.

What does not increase virtue or wealth is desire;
opposition to them is courting misfortune.

Acting on whims undermines character and dissipates capacity. When integrity disintegrates and resources dwindle, misfortune cannot be far off.

People who are exceedingly honest by nature
are hard to find.
One with integrity despises
supremacy gained dishonorably.

Confucius said, "To me, wealth and status wrongly gained are like ephemeral clouds."

A single fault eclipses
a multitude of virtues.

A scholar once asked a Zen master why people harp on a relatively minor flaw in an otherwise exemplary person. The Zen master said that it is precisely because the person is otherwise exemplary that a relatively minor flaw is particularly noticed.

Don't be aggressive
toward a great adversary.

Citing an ancient maxim, the *Tao Te Ching* says, "Let us not be aggressors, but defend."

Conduct should never be
excessive or remiss.

A Zen proverb says, "Going too far is as bad as not going far enough."

A lion does not graze on grass,
even if tormented by hunger.

A Zen proverb says, "An elephant does not walk a rabbit path."

Trust is to be preserved,
even at the cost of life.

Confucius said that a state could dispense with arms before food, and could dispense with food before trust. Questioned about dispensing with food before trust, Confucius explained, "There has always been death, but without trust it is impossible to stand."

A listener who betrays is abandoned,
even by his wife and children.

If people betray confidences, others will stop having confidence in them.

Ear should be lent
to what is meaningful and profitable,
even coming from a child.

The question to ask is whether something is useful, not where it came from. One of the greatest Zen masters said he would learn from anyone who was more enlightened, even a seven-year-old child; and he would give advice to anyone who was less enlightened, even a hundred-year-old elder.

The unbelievable should not be voiced,
even if it is true.

The Sufi master Ali said, "People oppose what they don't know anything about." Voicing something beyond the pale of current beliefs invariably incurs opposition and incites disturbance. This environmental condition is one reason for constructive use of discretion and tact.

Many good qualities are not to be disregarded
on account of a little flaw.
Flaws are commonly found even among the learned;
there is no jewel that does not break.

Because a minor flaw in an otherwise exemplary individual can distract the attention of ordinary thinkers, a good leader does not dwell morbidly on a weakness but restores duly constructive attention to the person's strengths.

Courtesy that is excessive
should never be trusted.

If courtesy seems forced rather than heartfelt, one wonders the reasons why.

In an adversary, even a friendly deed is hostile.
Even as it bows down, the beam of the pump
uses up the water in the well.

A "glad hand" of friendliness may be extended in order to take
something. It may be necessary to know and understand others well to
perceive their intentions.

One should not neglect the opinion of the good.
By association with those imbued with virtuous qualities,
even those lacking in such qualities come to have them.
Water in milk becomes like milk;
in alloy with gold, silver becomes golden.

The great Zen master Kuei-shan wrote, "Association with the good
is like walking through mist and dew; although your garments are not
drenched, in time they become imbued with moisture." Confucius said,
"Good people form associations for education and action."

The unenlightened seek to hurt benefactors.
Evildoers have no fear of criticism.

Biting the hand that feeds is a sign of ignorance; having no conscience is a sign of sociopathy.

The energetic subdue even the hostile;
prowess is the wealth of kings.
The indolent one has neither here nor hereafter;
opportunity is lost through lack of exertion.

Energy and ability can build nations; complacency and indifference
can ruin generations.

Useful resources should be recognized
as a fisherman does water.

An expert fisherman knows what fish live where. An expert leader knows what possibilities people and things may attain.

The suspicious are not to be trusted;
poison is always poison.

People who cannot trust cannot be trusted. At the very least, they will be suspicious of your motives in trusting them, and thus have no compunction about betraying your trust.

In the acquisition of wealth
there should be no association with enemies.
After having attained wealth,
one should not trust an enemy.

If you get ahead by compromising with people who are basically antagonistic to you, then you will compromise your liberty, security and integrity in the process of acquiring wealth. If you allow self-seekers to ingratiate themselves with you after you have already achieved success, it will be harder for you to use your wealth wisely.

A steady relationship is also based on wealth;
a friend should be protected,
even the son of an adversary.

Without resources, how could one protect a friend in need?

Until you see an adversary's weakness,
action or combat are to be avoided;
one should strike an enemy's weak spot.
One should not reveal one's own weakness;
adversaries aim at weak spots.

The Art of War says, "A skillful attack is one against which an enemy does not know where to defend, while a skillful defense is one against which an enemy does not know where to attack."

An enemy is not to be trusted,
even when you have him captive.

The Art of War says, "Be subtle, subtle even to the point of formless-ness; be mysterious, mysterious even to the point of soundlessness: thus you can control the enemy's fate."

Bad business on the part of one's own people
should be stopped:
for disgrace in their own people
brings pain to the high-minded;
damage to a single limb brings a person down.
Good conduct overcomes the enemy.

Within a large and complex operation, deviation from accepted norms may go uncorrected in isolated cases, counting on the overall integrity of the whole. This could lead to internal demoralization and external friction, possibly causing major losses by minor negligence. For an organization to be viable in a competitive society, it needs to main-tain acceptable and efficient standards of conducting its business.

The base are fond of dishonesty;
a good idea shouldn't be given to a base person—
they are not to be trusted.
A bad person causes injury,
even if treated well;
a forest fire burns even the sandalwood trees.

It is one thing when the base are known for their baseness, another when malevolence is deeply hidden. Chinese manuals of leadership and strategy give numerous ways of testing people's character, yet there is still a Zen saying: "The difficulty of knowing people is what ails sages." Learning who is worthy of confidence is a crucial task of leadership and a skill of individual self-government.

A person should never be disrespected.
One should not torment a person who can be forgiven.

Good leaders and good neighbors do not overlook the good in others, and they respect the need for human dignity. Even when people have made mistakes or gone wrong, it is better and more useful to seek redeeming qualities than to dwell on their errors.

Fools wish to voice aloud
the secret intimated by their superiors.

Those who breach the security of their own organizations endanger their own positions and lose the trust of others as well.

Devotion is manifested by its results.
The result of direction is dominion.
The fool finds it hard to give
even what is due.

The quality and degree of attention, care and concentration devoted to a task or an enterprise will be reflected in its fruition. When effort is directed correctly and effectively, then mastery can be attained. One who expects to reap rewards without expending due effort is not thinking realistically.

One who lacks firmness perishes,
even after attaining great dominion.
For one who lacks firmness,
there is neither the here and now
nor the hereafter.

When one can be easily swayed under the influence of external pressures or seductions, or if one can be destabilized by subjective wishes or fears, it is impossible to be resolute. Without firmness of will and resoluteness of action, one cannot succeed in either worldly endeavors or spiritual strivings.

Do not associate with bad people;
in the hands of a drunkard, even milk is despised.

Association with the wrong people fosters bad habits by learning through contact and also ruins one's reputation in the community. When one's behavior and character have become warped, and one is no longer trusted by decent people, failure and loss follow naturally.

What determines utility in crises at work is intelligence.

Prudence and forethought may not be enough to prevent the arising of unexpected difficulties. What counts in such circumstances is not regret and recrimination, but intelligent application to resolution of the problem.

Health comes from moderate eating:
No food should be eaten while digestion is incomplete,
whether it is wholesome or not.
Sickness does not approach one who digests food thoroughly.

A traditional Japanese prescription for good health is to eat only to the point where the stomach is 80 percent full. The prophet Muhammad said that a hypocrite eats enough for seven stomachs, while a believer eats only enough for one. Christian doctrine also refers to gluttony as one of the seven cardinal sins. Perhaps a similar caveat could be applied to all forms of consumption. Overconsumption leads to jading of taste, while jading leads to increased overconsumption and further waste. Ultimately wealth is consumed without enjoyment, pleasure or profit.

A growing disease in an aged body should not be overlooked.
Eating in a state of indigestion is harmful.
Sickness is even worse than an enemy.

A growing disease in an aged body may refer, besides the obvious meaning, to corruption in a long-established organization, system or society. Just as an aged body has less resistance to disease, so a complacent society may be lackadaisical about addressing decadent tendencies.

Eating in a state of indigestion is harmful to health because it increases indigestion, discomfort and general strain on the whole system. Roman aristocrats of imperial days used to eat as much as they could at banquets, then go vomit in the vomitorium and come back to eat their fill again. And again and again, it seems, perhaps until they passed out. Perhaps it is no wonder the Roman empire was overrun in time by hardier people from the north.

The wealth of Rome on which the imperial aristocrats wined and dined themselves silly was based on the wealth produced by their slaves and the peoples they conquered in Europe, the Middle East and Africa. Rome had the power to subdue and subjugate many peoples until the establishment so sickened itself by overconsumption that its imperial might crumbled away under the onslaughts of tribal warriors rising against their enfeebled masters. So for a body as powerful as the Roman empire, "sickness is even worse than an enemy."

Generosity goes with wealth.

Neglect of this principle was undoubtedly one of the symptoms of the illness that felled the Roman empire, and probably of every other empire in history as well. All empires fall in time, or they fall apart, because they were based on gross overconsumption by a relative few at the expense of the majority of people. Confucius said, "Those above secure their homes by kindness to those below."

The clever and the covetous are easy to deceive; intellect is veiled by craving.

This is also one of the basic principles of classical Chinese strategic philosophy. It is important to know how vulnerable others are to deceit in accord with their desires; it is even more important to know the level of one's own vulnerability to deception through wishful thinking.

Cynical people may be those who have had painful experiences through disappointment of hopes and consciously or unconsciously chose cynicism in the form of automatic, defensive rejection of hope itself. Cynics abandon hope without abandoning desire to take whatever immediate satisfactions can be gotten. They make this choice in preference to the more difficult undertaking of deliberate reexamination of the two-way relationship between fundamental hopes and effective realities.

When there is much work to do,
great reward should be made an inducement.

When rewards and penalties are used for motivation and restraint, it is axiomatic that they should be reliable, predictable and suited to the importance or gravity of the deed or misdeed, not the status of the person. The Master of the Hidden Storehouse said, "When trust is complete, the world is secure. When trust is lost, the world is dangerous. When the common people labor diligently and yet their money and goods run out, then contentious and antagonistic attitudes arise, and people do not trust each other.

"When people do not trust each other, this is due to unfairness in government practices. When there is unfairness in government practices, this is the fault of officials. When officials are at fault, penalties and rewards are unequal. When penalties and rewards are unequal, this means the leadership is not conscientious.

"When the leadership is conscientious, then penalties and rewards are uniform. When penalties and rewards are uniform, then officials obey the law. When officials obey the law, then order reigns. When order reigns, the common folk find their places and interact trustingly."

If people can trust that their services and achievements will be rewarded for their merit, then they can be motivated to do their best. If people suspect that sycophants and cronies will garner the lion's share of credit and profit, rarely will people not become cynical.

Work that is to be done by oneself alone
is to be examined.

Some things require collective effort, some things must be done alone. The first thing to examine is whether a particular task can be delegated, or calls for cooperation with others, or should be done by oneself alone. If it is something that one needs to take care of oneself, then there is no counting on information or feedback from others, so one has to be sure to take personal account of all factors relevant to the job, including the necessary knowledge, practical planning and continuous monitoring of progress all along the course of the task. Thus a task one is to do alone should be thoroughly examined from the start.

In fools, daring should be restrained.

The daring of the prudent is close to confidence, based on a foundation of knowledge and experience. The daring of the foolish is close to madness, based on a foundation of heedlessness and recklessness. There are times when daring may be necessary, in order to make progress or to break through an impasse of some kind. The daring of fools, however, seldom works out for the best. Even when it does seem to work out, that is not by virtue of the daring of fools, but by virtue of the luck of fools.

There's no arguing with fools;
to fools, one must speak like a fool.
Iron has to be cut by iron.

To try making sense by reasoning with a fool is itself foolish. Rationalize by means of the fool's brand of folly, however, and the fool may hear what you have to say.

Those who lack intelligence have no companion.

The Sufi master Ali said, "The richest of riches is intelligence, and the greatest poverty is stupidity. The loneliest isolation is conceit, and the most noble value is goodness of character."

The world is maintained by justice.

Socrates said, "It is by justice that the universals of the world exist, and its particulars cannot exist without it."

The Taoist Huainan Masters said, "Humanity and justice are the warp and woof of society; this never changes."

Justice and injustice follow even the departed.

The effects of justice and injustice continue even after the event; the good and evil people do throughout their lives outlive them in the end. Buddha said, "One who does evil suffers regret in this world and after death, regretful in both. One suffers regret knowing one has done wrong, and suffers more when gone to a state of misery. One who does good rejoices in this world and after death, joyful in both. One rejoices knowing one has done good, and rejoices even more when gone to a state of felicity."

Compassion is the birthground of justice; the roots of justice are truth and charity.

Compassion is the birthground of justice because understanding or commonality of feeling is what gives rise to consideration for others; and consideration for others, and by extension for society and humanity at large, is a basic ingredient of human motivation for doing justice. Truth and charity are roots of justice in that truth and charity are the avenues by which genuine needs are recognized and fulfilled; and recognition and fulfillment of real human needs are elemental functions of justice.

One overcomes the world with justice;
even death protects one who stands on justice.

When the Chinese philosopher Wen-tzu asked the Taoist sage Lao-tzu about justice, Lao-tzu said, "If you are in a superior position, you help the weak; if you are in a subordinate position, you maintain control over yourself. Don't indulge in your whims when you are successful, and don't get excitable when you are in straits. Follow reason uniformly, without bending it subjectively. This is called justice."

Where evil occurs as false justice,
there great contempt for true justice results.

When people see that the current operation of conventional organs and practices of justice in their society is actually resulting in manifest injustice, they may long for real justice, unless they have seen or heard of so many travesties of justice that they despair of real justice.

Then again, when people in positions of power use their authority to sanction personal whims to the detriment of the larger body of a society, their contempt for true justice is greatest of all.

Contempt for true justice can thus arise among both the victimized and the victimizers. This can result in violent confrontation, which under these conditions may be just as likely to be initiated from one side as the other and is probably even more likely to be initiated by both sides, each in its own way, both sides having lost faith in true justice, each in its own way.

Those whose destruction is imminent are recognized by temperament, determination and conduct.

People who are temperamental, willful and devious tend to lose the trust of others and wind up surrounded only by those who aim to exploit their temper, obsessiveness and craft.

Warped intelligence indicates self-destruction.

Typical modes of destructive misuse of intelligence include rationalization of unreasonable behavior, perpetrating and justifying dishonest behavior, and intentionally deceiving, attacking or confusing other people. Unfortunately, these phenomena are ordinarily more easily seen in retrospect than in prospect; perhaps the principle is emphasized so strongly in hopes that enough retrospective recognition might foster future perspective and foresight.

To vicious gossips, there is no secret.
Don't even listen to others' secrets.

Plato said, "One who pays attention to a statement is a confederate of the speaker." He also said, "Evil people look for people's faults, ignoring their good qualities, just as flies look for rotten parts of a body, ignoring the wholesome." Aristotle said, "A malicious person is an enemy to himself, so how can he be a friend to another?"

It is not right for a director to be an agent.

One who is in charge yet is dominated by the influence of others is not really in charge.

Do not be overbearing to your own people;
even a mother is bound to be abandoned if she is bad.

If one presumes upon a relationship and becomes imperious and abusive, alienation will follow. This can happen even in close blood relationships; mistreating people in personal, social or professional relationships results in rejection more readily yet.

Even one's own hand should be cut off if it is poisoned;
while a benefactor is kin, even if a stranger.

Jesus said that if your hand offends you, then you should cut it off, for it is better to lose a hand than for the whole body to go to hell. Pythagoras said that a neighbor nearby is more helpful than a brother far away; Ali said that kinship is more in need of friendship than friendship is of kinship.

There is no trusting thieves.

Zen lore warns against treating a thief like a son. There is a specific admonition against "giving a ladder to a thief," or unwittingly giving assistance to the dishonest. A proverb says, "Bring in a wolf, and it'll crap in the house."

Even when there are no problems, it won't do to be negligent. Even a small defect can prevent success.

A Chinese maxim says, "When safe, don't forget about danger." A Zen proverb says, "The spoils of victory are ruined by celebration." Too much enjoyment of the feeling of success and security can undermine attentiveness to subtle changes in external conditions, leading to neglect of adaptive inner changes, ultimately producing gaps in which vulnerabilities and problems tend to arise.

One should acquire wealth like an immortal;
the wealthy one is respected by all;
the world does not think much of one without wealth,
even a great chieftain.
Poverty, after all, is a living death for a person.

This is practical observation of what happens in the world; it is social economics, not ideological philosophy. Sufi master Ali noted, "The rich man is at home even when abroad; the pauper is a stranger in his hometown."

An ugly man with wealth is handsome;
even if he is ungenerous,
seekers do not forsake the wealthy man;
the low born, if rich, is superior to the high born.

This is also observation, not philosophy; and these observations are at least as true today, in practical terms, as they were when they were written. Chandragupta Maurya, who became emperor of the greatest Indian empire of all time, is supposed to have been a lowly cowherd and soldier before he met the pundit Kauthilya, who taught him the art of wealth and the conduct of kings.

An ignoble man has no fear of dishonor;
intelligent people have no fear for their livelihood.
There is no fear of objects for those with controlled senses;
there is no fear of death for those
who have accomplished their purpose.

Ignoble people have no fear of dishonor, so no one can trust them. Intelligent people have no fear for their livelihood, so no one need worry about them. Those with controlled senses have no fear of objects, so no one can do anything to influence them. Those who have accomplished their purpose have no fear of death, so no one can do anything to intimidate them.

A good man considers himself rich
when everyone is rich.

A good man considers himself rich when everyone is rich because he feels his own riches oblige him to give to the needy. When everyone is rich, wealth does not drain away, but can be accumulated and redeployed for development of other forms of enrichment.

No interest should be taken in the possessions of others;
interest in others' property is the root of ruination.
An object belonging to another should not be taken,
even a stalk of straw;
taking away others' things
is the cause of loss of one's own things—
no noose is higher than thieving.

When there is no taking interest in others' possessions, feelings of envy or rivalry cannot arise. In most societies, needy people generally consider it better to beg than to steal; and most thieves, it seems, are generally not needy people, but greedy people. What happens to them in the end depends on whether they were more greedy than needy or more needy than greedy.

Even gruel sustains life, if available in time;
medicine is of no use to the dead.
At the same time, you yourself
are the opportunity for sovereignty.

It may be better to make do with less than to hold out for more if time is of the essence. If minimum needs are not fulfilled in time, there is no use in hoping for something better. Therefore it is important to recognize necessities and possibilities. Most of all, it is essential to take responsibility for one's own needs and capacities, to recognize in one's own being the opportunity for competence, self-mastery and fulfillment.

The sciences of the base-minded
are harnessed to evil deeds.
Drinking milk increases poison in a snake;
it doesn't turn to ambrosia.

From this point of view, the notion that science and religion are inherently incompatible, or the notion that science and the humanities are separate domains, would seem to be rooted in pessimistic assumptions about morality and ability that are already too limited for practical, constructive use.

The popular image of the evil "mad scientist" who tries to control the world or destroy the world is considered fictional, no doubt, because there are many scientists who are not mad. Yet relatively sane scientists and thinkers may find no practical choice but to work in the employ of organizations that are actually trying to control the world in one way or another, and are indeed succeeding in destroying the world in several dimensions, without anyone ordinarily thinking that is actually madness. To the mind habituated to such a situation, it is ordinarily not considered pathological; it is regarded as nothing more or less than the way things are.

Most people are not confronted with scientific statistics day in and day out, but if they were made to become constantly conscious of the enormity of environmental pollution and destruction on the face of the earth, and of the vastness of the amount of productivity and wealth that has been and is being funneled into destructive power, power so immense that it would be sufficient to annihilate every human being in existence several times over, then people would probably either consider that madness or they would soon go mad themselves under the duress of this realization.

There is no wealth like grain, there is no enemy like hunger.

Hunger undermines both physical and mental health. There is no telling what people may do when they get too hungry too often. They easily get sick, and they might go crazy.

Grain and wealth can be expressed by the same word in Sanskrit, for grain is a basic form of wealth. Grain is perhaps the most prolific and economical source of human food energy, far more efficient than harvesting energy from meat. The Hindu custom of eating grain as the staple of the diet and not eating the meat of cattle is not superstition, but hygiene and economics.

One who keeps up impropriety goes hungry;
there's nothing the hungry will not eat.

People who continue to misbehave toward others wind up being abandoned and shunned. Then they will be in the position of "beggars can't be choosers."

The senses subject you to old age.

The *Tao Te Ching* says, "Colors blind people's eyes; sounds deafen their ears; flavors spoil people's palates; the chase and the hunt craze people's minds."

Livelihood should be earned
from a compassionate employer;
one who works for someone who's greedy
fans a firefly in hopes of fire.
One should choose an employer who's judicious.

Employers screen potential employees; workers should also screen potential employers. If workers see they have no prospects of enrichment or advancement by dint of personal effort because the ownership takes the profits in bonuses and dividends, then the workers will lack motivation to do anything more than get by. If workers see that a firm is unstable because of a quirky management or directorate, then they cannot be deeply committed to the enterprise. The *Tao Te Ching* says, "Those who embody nobility to act for the sake of the world seem to be able to draw the world to them, while those who embody love to act for the sake of the world seem to be worthy of the trust of the world."

Longevity, reputation and virtue wane
by approaching those who should not be approached.

Associating with the wrong people can lead to unhealthy habits, disrespect and bad morals.

There is no enemy like ego.

Nothing helps you deceive yourself like your ego; nothing helps others manipulate you like your ego. If you think you are invulnerable to deception and manipulation, that too is a suggestion of your ego.

Don't complain of an enemy in company;
it is pleasant to hear of an enemy's distress.

When you complain, you are expressing your own distress; thus you please your enemy by showing how distressed you are.

Intelligence is not found in the ne'er-do-well;
the advice of a pauper is not taken, even if it is good.
A pauper is disrespected, even by his own wife;
bees do not approach a mango tree if it has no flowers.

It is expected that one with intelligence would not be a habitual failure. It is not expected that someone who shows a lack of resourcefulness could have any good advice to give. One who lacks resourcefulness and proves to be a habitual failure is not disrespected because of social prejudice, but because of habitual failure and lack of resourcefulness. One who cannot contribute anything to others, even on the level of the nuclear family, will normally be considered a liability anywhere.

Knowledge is wealth for the poor;
knowledge cannot be taken by thieves.

The Sufi master Ali said, "Knowledge is better than wealth. Knowledge protects you, while you protect wealth. Wealth is diminished by spending, while knowledge grows by use."

One who acts for the benefit of others is a good person.

This may seem to be a truism, but then again it is possible for some forms of pious behavior to become so ritualized as to lose constructive relevance to society at large. Conceptions of good may also differ, and even conflict, so the practical thinker evaluates the actual effect of action, whatever the rationale.

Learning means tranquility of the senses.
The prod of learning turns one away from ignorant behavior.

Learning that results in clear understanding leads to the serenity of certitude with freedom from doubt, and the ability to recognize and consider the range of potential meanings and consequences of actions.

The knowledge of the base-minded is not worth acquiring.
Barbaric speech should not be learned.
Good manners should be acquired,
even those of foreigners.

If the knowledge of base-minded people were uplifting, then they wouldn't be base-minded. If barbaric speech could win people over, it wouldn't be considered barbaric. If considerate behavior were nothing but culture-specific ritual, then people of different backgrounds could never get along with each other.

Don't envy character;
a good quality should be learned,
even from an enemy:
ambrosia can be obtained from poison.

It is self-defeating to envy another's character, for envy itself degrades one's own character. Confucius said he could find a teacher even in a group of three people: when he saw something good, he would emulate it himself; and when he saw something bad, he would correct it in himself.

One should practice the conduct of the upright
and never overstep bounds.

The Sufi master Ali said, "You will find the ignorant either remiss or excessive."

A jewel of a man has no price;
there is no jewel like a jewel of a woman;
a jewel is really hard to find.

In Sanskrit convention, a jewel is used to represent the finest example of something. The best men cannot be bought, the best women are beyond compare. If jewels could readily be found all over the place, they would not be called jewels.

Ill repute is the fear of fears.

Social beings depend on each other and on the groups with which they are associated. That is why ostracization is a classical method of punishment in human societies. The fear of ill repute is ultimately the fear of ostracization, which is frightening because it deprives the individual of social, economic and psychological security. According to the Buddhist *Flower Ornament Scripture,* fear of ill repute is banished only when fear of death itself is transcended.

There is no attainment of learning for the lazy.

In the basic Mahayana Buddhist system of education, diligence is the fourth requirement for enlightenment, after charity, morality and patience, because the many practices involved in waking the whole mind cannot be successfully performed without diligence.

Once when Confucius saw a student sleeping in the daytime, he remarked, "Rotten wood cannot be carved, a manure wall cannot be plastered. What admonition is there for me to give?"

One who wants flowers does not water a withered tree;
an undertaking without resources
is no different from plowing the sand.

Don't spend time, money and effort on a project that you should realize cannot in the nature of things yield sufficient return to make it worthwhile. While it may seem that no one would ever undertake such a project to begin with, nevertheless it does happen, whether because of wishful thinking, or because of the momentum of certain habits, or because of misperception of realities.

Practical philosophers of classical times would sometimes cite simple common sense as a way of jarring their listeners into asking themselves whether they really had any common sense and whether something else, perhaps such as superstition, custom or other automatic behavior, might not take over their thinking from time to time.

The success of a task is indicated by the operative causes;
indications of operative causes are better than astrology.
There is no astrology for someone in a hurry.

Buddhist practical philosophy also emphasizes the understanding of causality, including the understanding that causality cannot be understood in reality by a fixed system of interpretation. People often blunder when they want fortune cookie explanations of events and advice for the future because it seems easier that way. The idea of being given guaranteed formulas can be more attractive than the idea of taking the time and effort to observe causal conditions, gathering potentially useful information and knowledge, and sharpening perceptions.

Where there is familiarity, faults are not concealed.

No doubt this is the reason why "familiarity breeds contempt." It also means that cultivating familiarity is a tool of spies and other secret agents, who seek to discover the faults of others as a way of life.

One who is himself impure is suspicious of others.

A Chinese saying has it, "Doubt in the mind, ghosts in the dark." Common sense often tells people that those who are most strident in condemning others may simply be those who feel the most need to justify themselves.

It is hard to overcome innate disposition.

An Irish proverb says, "Heredity will come through the claws, and the hound will pursue the hare." But difficulty is not impossibility. Another Irish maxim says, "A man is better than his birth."

Let the penalty fit the offense,
let the response fit the remark.
Let adornment accord with circumstances,
let conduct accord with the community.
Let the undertaking suit the task,
let the gift befit the receiver.

According to the Taoist Huainan Masters, "A wise ruler employs people the way a skilled craftsman works with wood. There is an appropriate use for everything, great and small, long and short; there is an application for both the ruler and the compass, for the square and the round."

The Huainan Masters also said, "People have their specific talents; things have their specific forms. Therefore petty-minded policies will inevitably cause loss of the overall integrity of society."

Excessive courtesy is suspect.

The Taoist classic *Tao Te Ching* says, "Higher courtesy is done, but no one responds to it; so there is forceful repetition." It also says, "Courtesy comes after loss of the sense of duty; manners mean loyalty and trust are thin, and disarray is beginning."

A fool does not see fault in himself; he only sees fault in others.

Buddhism, Taoism and Confucianism teach people to look for faults in themselves when they see them in others. This exercise is used to improve disposition and character in oneself, and to develop empathy and compassion for others.

With courtesy comes deceit.
Courtesy is offering the desirable and the preferable.
Excessive politeness from longtime acquaintances is suspect.

When you are more courteous to people than their own behavior deserves, they may deceive themselves into thinking you respect them more than you actually do. When you are more polite to people than your relationship requires, they may wonder what you are thinking.

A single milk-making cow is better than a thousand dogs.

Where quality or utility are required, quantity is no substitute for either.

A pigeon today is better than a peacock tomorrow.

One thing may seem more desirable, but something else may be more possible. Perceiving this distinction helps eliminate confusion in decision making.

Too much togetherness causes trouble.

This may be because familiarity breeds contempt or because people are vulnerable to manipulation when their personal weaknesses are known to others.

The one free of anger overcomes all.

In Buddhist practical philosophy, anger is considered one of the most basic poisons of the human mind.

When angry at a wrongdoer,
it is the anger at which one should be angry.

Anger injures the body and mind, and it is not a necessary part of recognizing and repudiating wrong. Anger at wrongdoing causes self-injury and, if taken to extremes, may lead the angry themselves into wrongdoing.

Don't argue with the wise or the foolish,
or with friends, teachers or loved ones.

It is foolish to argue with the wise, even more foolish to argue with fools. It is painful to argue with friends, presumptuous to argue with teachers and graceless to argue with loved ones.

There is no supremacy without fiendish determination.

This aphorism is not necessarily a recommendation for fiendish determination or a recommendation to struggle for supremacy. What it may suggest is to be sure to assess ambitions rationally, not just entertain them wishfully or pursue them blindly. For maximum economy of effort, it helps to think about aims in terms of costs as well as rewards. It may seem attractive to get ahead of others; it may seem less attractive to have to be watching one's back at all times.

It is no trouble for the wealthy to do good deeds;
a journey is no trouble for those who have a vehicle.

Perhaps this may mean that it is simply rational, nothing wonderful, when wealthy people fund charitable enterprises.

One should be employed where one is skillful.

The Taoist Huainan Masters said, "When there is no discrimination, and each individual finds a suitable way of life, then the world is equalized; no one dominates another. Sages find work for all of them, so no abilities are wasted."

The mother is the most important of all teachers.
The mother is to be supported in all conditions of age.

The mother's education begins while the child is in the womb, imprinting her offspring's body with the effects of her moods, thoughts and actions. After birth, when infants are distressed by life outside the womb, the mother must identify the particular need and attend to it; without this form of teaching conveying to them a sense of order in the world, infants can lose hope and become autistic at a prearticulate stage. The first three years of life, in which the primary caregiver is normally the mother, are believed to create such a deep impression on an individual as to exert a lifelong influence. There is literally no calculating the debt that is owed to mothers.

Erudition is clothed in manners of speaking.

The Taoist Master of Demon Valley said, "When you have examined people's mentalities, intentions and thoughts, and have gotten to know what they like and dislike, then you can speak of what is important to them, using intoxicating and arresting expressions to hook into the inclinations and thereby hold them and attract them."

The ornament of women is modesty,
the ornament of intellectuals is learning,
the ornament of everyone is justice.

The ornament of ornaments
is knowledge combined with humility.

The Sufi master Ali said that there is no faith like modesty and patience, no legacy like culture, no worship like discharge of obligations, no nobility like knowledge and no prestige like humility.

When the children are virtuous,
the home is paradise.
Children should be given complete education.

A complete education would include learning in the bases of virtue. Virtue has the meaning of morality and also the meaning of efficacy. By understanding the logical principles and effects of moral standards in action, it may be possible to attain successful effectiveness at ethical ways of living and working, resulting in an enhanced sense of security and well-being.

One whose destruction is imminent
does not listen to good advice.

One whose destruction is imminent may have already made a habit of not listening to good advice. When things are cracking up or crumbling down, anxiety and hurry will not make a habitually heedless person more sober and attentive. Ali said there is no support surer than consultation, and also that, "One who cautions you is as one who brings you good news."

As long as we have bodies,
there will never be no pleasure or pain.

The *Tao Te Ching* says, "The reason we have troubles is that we have bodies; if we had no bodies, what troubles would we have?"

Pleasure and pain follow one who makes them,
as children do their mother.

The Buddha said, "If one speaks or acts with a corrupt mind, misery will follow, as the wheel of a cart follows the foot of the ox. . . . If one speaks or acts with a pure mind, happiness will follow, like the shadow that never departs."

Even the smallest favor is deemed enormous
by the good person.

Taking favors for granted means loss of appreciation, and eventually loss of favor. Counting blessings, in contrast, no matter how small, is a way to develop a positive attitude and a constructive approach toward the experience of life.

No favor is due the dishonest.

Helping people who hurt others is tantamount to helping to hurt others.

Fearful of having to requite a favor,
the ignoble one turns hostile.

Those who want to get but don't want to give will usually find for themselves an excuse that they prefer over recognition of their own self-centered moral sloth. Using hostility to provoke hostility is one manner of creating an excuse for oneself that can be attempted with no moral or intellectual resources at all, fabricating as it does a sense of self-righteousness with the greatest of ease, involving no constructive effort.

The noble one does not neglect to requite even the smallest of favors.

One of the disciples of Confucius used to say, "Neither causing harm nor being importunate—how can this not be good?" Confucius rejoined, "How can this way be enough to be considered good?"

Divinity should never be disrespected.

In Hindu pantheism, everything is the face of God. In Hindu transcendentalism, God is the ultimate source and goal of every soul. In Islamic Arabic, the word for disbelief or rejection of the Divinity also means ingratitude. Everything in nature, including opportunity and choice, everything in the livelihood of humanity, is said to be a "sign of

God." From this point of view, an ungrateful attitude toward life, be it presumption or be it bitterness, is considered evident infidelity to the source and meaning of life itself.

There is no light like the eye, for the eye is the guide of beings.

Jesus Christ said the eye is the light of the body. The mind is called an eye, for people are led by what their minds perceive. According to Buddhists, there are five eyes. There is the eye of mortal sense, the eye of extrasensory perception, the eye of wisdom, the eye of objective reality and the enlightened eye comprehending all of these.

Don't piss in the water.

Environmentalism in ancient times is documented in classical Chinese literature of about the same era as this Sanskrit text. It could be argued, naturally, that this aphorism is a metaphor for similar principles in emotional, social and professional life.

As the body, so the consciousness.
As the intelligence, so the prowess.

Things that afflict the body stress consciousness with repulsion. Things that please the body stress consciousness with attraction. No life is exempt from either of these things in some form or another. The ability to employ the energy of this stress constructively depends on understanding its mechanism and knowing good measure.

Don't throw fire into fire.

When there is friction in a situation, venting anger will only make it worse.

One should follow what is right at all times.
What is wholesome and true leads to felicity.

Confucius said, "If your words are truthful and your actions are in earnest, they will be effective even in foreign countries. If your words are not truthful and your actions are not in earnest, do you think they would be effective even in your homeland?" Buddha said, "Energetic, alert, pure in deed, careful in action, self-controlled, living in accord with truth, the vigilant one will rise in repute." The *Tao Te Ching* says, "Build up virtue, and you master all."

There is no austerity greater than truth.
Truth leads to felicity;
the world is sustained by truth.
There is no fall worse than falsehood.

Truth is austerity in that it means abstention from wishful thinking and self-serving bias. Buddha said, "The abstinence of the ignorant is worth less than a sixteenth part of those who have integrated all truths." He also said, "One who is deluded and ignorant does not become a sage by silence; but the sage is the wise one who, holding the scale, takes to what is best." There is rigor in truth; but also well-being and peace of mind.

Don't get involved in villainy;
a villain has no friends.

Sufi master Ali, who was also the caliph, once said when a trouble-maker was brought before him, "There is no welcome for a face seen only on bad occasions."

Worldly subsistence troubles the pauper.

This appears to be an obvious truism. The point seems to be that if one does not take care of worldly subsistence in time, one will be too distracted and preoccupied to accomplish anything else. No doubt it was for this reason that in the traditional Aryan social system there were four stages of life: in the first stage, the main focus was education; in the second stage, the main focus was the establishment of livelihood; in the third stage, the main focus was marriage, family and enjoyment of life; in the fourth stage, the main focus was transcendence of the world and attainment of spiritual liberation.

There appears to be plenty of evidence that personal and social stagnation are caused by demanding the enjoyments of the third stage of life without having developed responsibility and capability in the first and second. Religious frustration can also be caused by trying to work on the fourth stage without having adequate experience of the first three stages of life.

The superhero is the heroic giver.

The heroic image of giving, by which it was recommended to warrior chieftains, was shared by classical cultures all over the world. In old Irish culture, which was cognate with Indian Hindu culture, generosity was expected of leadership, and a man was not judged by what he had so much as by what he gave.

Culture is an ornament for all;
even one who is not well born
can be superior to the well born
by virtue of training.

This aphorism is one piece of evidence that the so-called caste system of the Aryans was originally not so rigid as to exclude social mobility. While there were regional and temporal variations, it was evidently not until long after Kauthilya's time that the Indian caste system became generally sclerotic. A parallel class system in Ireland, whose language is related to Sanskrit and whose classical culture came from the same source as Hindu culture, shows a similar pattern of early flexibility later rigidified, yet always modified, as in this aphorism of Kauthilya, by the traditional maxim that "a man is better than his birth," meaning that people of all stations in life could improve their condition in life by education and training.

Life span is enhanced through good conduct, and so is reputation.

Good conduct enhances the life span through the benefit of moderation as well as reduction of friction, anxiety and other forms of stress that result from disharmony. A good reputation also contributes to this well-being by minimizing interpersonal resistance in the social and professional environment.

Don't say something useless, even if it is nice.

The Master of Demon Valley said, "The mouth is the door of the mind, the mind is the host of the spirit. Will, intention, joy, desire, thought, worry, knowledge and planning all go in and out through the door." One of the first secrets of success, according to this ancient leadership manual, is to learn to open and close that door at the appropriate times.

Don't go along with an isolated individual,
one who is opposed by many people.

The result of going along with an isolated individual who is opposed by many people is subjection to isolation and opposition. Even if misery loves company, such an alliance seems to be of no real worth to either party in the long run. The first question to ask might be why the individual is isolated and opposed to begin with.

Don't cast your lot with bad people;
don't join up with the successful
if they are base minded.

Even if dishonest people seem to be successful, that is not good enough reason to team up with them. Not only will association with bad people cause others to turn against you, making your place in the world inherently precarious, there is also nothing to stop what you thought was your team from leaving you holding the bag when trouble comes. Base-minded people who are successful at a particular time may, after all, have gotten where they are by deception and backstabbing all along. Connection with people of that nature ultimately leaves you without adequate security or reliable support for lasting success in the world, even if you think for a time that you are getting advantages from working with them.

Debts, enemies and illnesses
should be eliminated completely.

Indebtedness, enmity and sickness all have ways of compounding if they are left unattended.

To act in accord with well-being
is an elixir of life for a person.

This aphorism may seem like a truism, but it raises the questions of what well-being really is and what is actually conducive to well-being. Too much concern for gain can result in loss; excessive striving for benefit can cause harm. Trying too hard to get ahead or improve one's situation may result in anxiety and stress that damage health and shorten the life span.

Petitioners should not be treated with contempt.

You may or may not be able to fulfill a request, but there is no reason to look down on the person or the need. You may find yourself in the position of a petitioner yourself someday.

Having incited an evil act, the mean man derides the one who did it.

This is a useful illustration of meanness, whose main ingredients include weakness and cowardice. The word "mean" is commonly used in colloquial English in the sense of vicious or nasty, in literary English in the sense of base or ignoble. This Sanskrit aphorism illustrates the functional connection between baseness and viciousness in the corrupt personality.

An ingrate cannot avoid hell.

Ingrates go to hell when their habitual failure to appreciate goodness accumulates into a critical mass, producing a sensation of bitterness and discontent that never goes away but fluctuates between chronic and intense manifestations.

Growth and decline depend on the tongue;
the tongue is a storehouse of both poison and elixir.
One who speaks pleasantly has no enemy.
Even if not true, hard words remain a long time.
Nothing offensive to a ruler should be voiced;
they are pleased by musical speech that is delightful to hear.

On the art of persuasion, the Master of Demon Valley says, "When speaking with those who are in a positive mood, go by the exalted and the lofty; when speaking with those who are in a negative mood, go by the humble and the small. Seek the small by lowliness, seek the great by loftiness. Follow this procedure, and what you say can be expressed anywhere, will penetrate anywhere and can suit any situation. It will thereby be possible to persuade individuals, to persuade families, to persuade the world."

One who is motivated by personal duty has integrity.

Confucius said, "Ideal people understand things in terms of duty; lesser people understand things in terms of profit."

A beggar has no dignity.

Muhammad the Prophet said, "If any of you takes a rope and gets up early and goes into the mountains and cuts firewood and sells it, and eats from this and gives charity from this, that is better for you than to ask of others."

Even an enemy should not be caused to lose his livelihood.

When people are deprived of a means of livelihood, that not only hurts them and their families, but also drains others on whom they become dependent. Even in conflict with enemies, to treat them in this way would be counterproductive because it would inevitably create an inherent source of instability, undermining general peace and well-being.

Don't anger an elephant
while wielding only a castor-bean plant.
Even the biggest cotton tree is no tying post for an elephant.
No matter how tall, a softwood tree cannot make clubs.
No matter how bright, a firefly is not fire.

According to the classic Chinese *Art of War* by Sun Tzu, "If you know others and know yourself, you will not be imperiled in a hundred battles."

Size is not a basis of virtue.

Virtue means efficacy. A small-scale operation may be more efficient than a large one.

As is the seed, so is the fruit.
Awareness is in accord with learning.
As is the family, so is the behavior.
A cultivated nimb tree does not become
a fragrant mango tree.

A nimb tree *(Azadirachta indica)* has bitter fruit by nature. What we get out of an undertaking depends on what we put into it. How we think and view the world depends on how we have been socialized and trained. How we normally behave depends on the examples we learned to consider normal in our formative years. Cultivation can have some effect, but it cannot change basic character.

Don't abandon happiness that has come to you.
One comes upon sorrow by oneself.

The Sufi master Ali said, "Take of the world what comes to you, and turn away from what turns away from you." He added, "If you cannot do this, at least be decent in seeking."

There should be no night rambling;
and one should not sleep only half the night.

The *I Ching* says, "Ideal people go inside and rest when the sun goes down."

One should look into reality
with the help of those with knowledge.

Without the help of those with knowledge, there is the danger of being impeded by subjective bias.

One should not enter the house of another without reason.

Recognition of the right to privacy and quiet enjoyment of home seems to be fundamental to individual freedom, civil liberty and domestic tranquility.

People do wrong even though they are aware of it.

Education, public opinion and common sense may not be sufficient to eliminate wrongdoing and crime.

Public conduct is headed by education;
where there is no education,
one should follow the ways of the learned.
There is no education more important than conduct.

When moral education is clearly at variance with the conduct of leaders of society, the body public subjected to contradictory impacts may become cynical, disillusioned and disaffected, losing respect for both leadership and education. The Taoist Huainan Masters said, "When people are influenced by their rulers, they follow what the rulers do, not what they say." Confucius said, "If you are personally upright, things get done without any orders being given. If you are not personally upright, no one will obey, even if you do give orders."

With spies for eyes,
a ruler sees even the distant.

The Huainan Masters said, "A ruler who does not descend from the upper part of the temple yet knows beyond the four seas is one who recognizes things by means of things and knows people by means of people. There is no limit to what accumulated power can lift. Whatever is done by the knowledge of many succeeds."

The Huainan Masters also said, "If you ride on the knowledge of the multitude, it is easy to gain dominion; if you use only your own mind, you cannot even preserve yourself."

The Huainan Masters also said, "Leaders see with the eyes of the whole nation, hear with the ears of the whole nation, think with the knowledge of the whole nation and move with the strength of the whole nation. For this reason, the directives of the leaders reach all the way to the lower echelons, while the feelings of the masses come to the notice of the leaders."

Society goes along
with what has already happened.

Repetition of the familiar and development of habits are characteristic actions of the brain, both individual and collective. This is often

useful to a certain point, like a kind of automatic pilot; but it may interfere with creative thought and action needed to adapt to changes.

One should not speak ill of anyone
on whom one is dependent.

It is common sense not to bite the hand that feeds you. It also makes
sense to consider the variety and extent of the whole range of inter-
dependent relationships, near and far, involved in the operation of the
world of everyday life: the sources of supplies and services; the sources of
social roots; the sources of education, gainful employment and recreation
on which people depend for their livelihood and liveliness.

The essence of discipline
is control of the faculties.

There are different forms of discipline, according to the inner and
outer conditions of society, but the essence of discipline itself is to master one's own faculties. The concept of discipline seems to have picked
up some baggage over the ages, apparently due to the visibility of its
exaggerations into monolithic authoritarianism and suppression of the

individual. The original concept of discipline illustrated in this apho-rism is quintessentially individualistic, in that control of one's own fac-ulties enables one to be independent of control by manipulation of either or both the internal and external environment.

A paradisical state is not permanent;
it lasts only as long as the result of virtues:
and there is no misery worse
than fall from a paradisical state.

According to Buddhist teaching, virtue without wisdom has three phases of negative consequences. The first phase is when good deeds are done in hopes of reward, distracting people from clarifying the essence of mind. The second phase is when pleasurable states that develop as results of good deeds become objects of attachment and possessiveness. The third phase is when the pleasurable states are worn out, while habitua-tion to them remains; this gap between actuality and conditioned expec-tation produces extra misery.

Liberation is the cure of sorrows.

Buddha said, "Be free of the past, be free of the future, be free of the meantime; be transcendent. When your mind is completely liberated, you no longer suffer birth and old age."

The enmity of the noble is better than the allegiance of the ignoble.

From the enmity of the noble one may learn to recognize one's own mistakes and faults; by the allegiance of the ignoble one may learn to disguise one's own mistakes and faults.

Hard words destroy the family.

Plato said, "It behooves those who take the young to task to leave them room for excuse, lest they drive them to be hardened by too much rebuke."

There is no greater pleasure
than contact with one's children.

People today might say this depends on the quality of one's relationship with one's children, but then again, it doesn't take that much to surpass the pleasure of abandonment.

In an argument,
keep justice in mind.

Don't get carried away by emotion or confused by verbal maneuvering; just pursue what is right and true.

When at leisure, one should think
of what is to be done.

This is the way to keep on top and ahead of things. If leisure is all used up in rest and diversion, and none is given to leisurely reflection and creative thinking, this can produce exaggerated cycles of lethargy and tension, thus reducing the recuperative value of leisure as well as the effectiveness of renewal in its aftermath.

One whose destruction is imminent thinks of bad plans.

It is often hard to think straight when hard pressed. That is no doubt why it is better to think ahead when there is free time, as the previous aphorism recommends. Strategies formulated on the spot in moments of crisis and states of high anxiety are too often distorted by emotion, or based on too narrowly focused attention, to be effective in practice.

For one who needs milk, what is the use of an elephant?

A common feature of bad planning is reliance on quantitative abundance in place of qualitative exactitude.

There is no power of subjection
equal to a gift.

Using debt or gratitude to influence or manipulate people is an insidious practice known in the Japanese vernacular as "making someone wear gratitude." An early Muslim said, "In the lifetime of the Prophet, a gift was a gift. Today, it is a bribe."

One should not long for that
which is at the disposition of another.
Only an immature person enjoys ill-gotten gains;
bitter fruit is eaten only by crows.

Coveting what is rightfully at the disposal of others creates psychological complications; taking what is rightfully at the disposal of others, whether by stealth, by deception or by force, creates social complications.

An ocean does not quench thirst.

A successful individual may be surrounded by many people in good times, but they may all prove useless when a real need arises.

Even grains of sand stick by their own kind:
the wholesome do not enjoy
the company of the unwholesome;
a swan does not frequent a burning-ground.

People may put on appearances to make a certain impression on others, but their habitual associations will ultimately reveal their true character.

The world goes on for the sake of wealth:
the world is bound by wishful expectation,
but prosperity does not abide with those

given to wishful expectation.
There is no firmness in those
given to wishful expectation.

When Confucius remarked that he had never seen a person who was firm, one of his students mentioned someone as an example. Confucius retorted, "He is covetous—how can he be firm?"

Death is better than meanness.

Mean people also have to die. The quality of mean-spirited living, however, whether considered in terms of cause or in terms of effect, might make it seem that death would be better.

Desire drives away shame.

Mencius said that people should have a sense of shame in order to reach the point where they have nothing to be ashamed of. This element of personal cultivation naturally affects professional life as well.

Confucius said, "Can an ignoble man serve the government? No. He worries about getting something, and once he has got, he worries about losing it. As long as he worries about losing, there's no telling what he might do."

One should not praise oneself.

A̲li said, "The loneliest isolation is conceit."

One should not sleep by day.

B̲uddha said, "People who are negligent are as if dead."

**One who is blinded by prosperity
does not even see what is at hand,
or listen to a good word.**

The *Tao Te Ching* says, "To keep on filling is not as good as stopping. . . . Though gold and jewels fill their houses, no one can keep them. When the rich upper classes are haughty, their legacy indicts them."

A guest is to be treated properly.

Hospitality is a basic thread of the fabric of many traditional societies. In old Irish culture, the westernmost relative of Hindu culture, hospitality was considered so fundamental that free public hospitality houses were official institutions.

An enemy appears to be a friend;
a mirage appears to be water.

According to the Chinese warrior-philosopher Sun Tzu, subterfuge and deception are normal practices in strategic arts.

Pseudoscience seduces the ignorant.

Kauthilya also said, "Indications of operative causes are better than astrology." Brahmins of India and druids of Ireland, heirs of a common tradition of high antiquity, both included natural sciences among their domains of study. The idea of scientific objectivity is not something new, and not specifically Western, just as pseudoscience is not confined to premodern societies. Numerous sages and prophets in various ancient cultures opposed superstition, often at considerable cost to themselves. Confucius, it is said, "did not talk about strange things, powers, chaos or the spiritual." Abraham, Moses, Buddha and Muhammad also discouraged popular superstitions of their times.

The company of the good is paradise.
The noble one thinks of others as self.

Buddha said, "The sight of the noble is good, association with them is always happy. One who never sees fools will be happy forever."

Buddha also said, "Follow one who is wise, insightful, learned, enduring, dutiful, noble, a genuine human being, authentically intelligent."

One's place is where one can live happily.

The Huainan Masters said, "Let individuals suit their natures, be secure in their abodes, live as best they can and exercise their capabilities." The *Tao Te Ching* speaks of a state in which people can "relish their food, like their clothes, are comfortable in their ways and enjoy their work."

There is no salvation for one who destroys trust.

Confucius considered trust the most basic ingredient of society. He said that it is more important even than food and armament because nothing constructive can be done without trust.

The honorable man considers the suffering of dependents as his own.

When a successful man thought himself more important than those below him in rank, Muhammad the Prophet said to him, "Are you made triumphant and provided sustenance except by the powerless among you?"

The Prophet also said, "You see the believers in their mutual kindness, love and sympathy, as if they were a single body. When one of its members is ailing, the rest of the body joins it in sleeplessness and fever."

The ignoble man hides what is in his heart and speaks of something else.

When asked how to work for rulers, Confucius replied, "Don't deceive them, even if you have to offend them."

An irrational man is equivalent to a demon.

With someone who allows no possibility of reasonable interaction or rational discourse, such that there is no way to predict the effect and outcome of one's own behavior, one will have a devil of a time dealing gracefully. It may very well be that this is precisely the reason why some people will actually choose irrationality under certain circumstances. When people seem unreasonable, therefore, it may be useful to see whether they are truly irrational or strategically so. It would probably be useful to check one's own rationality as well.

One should not travel unaccompanied.

Company on the road can improve morale and multiply resources for dealing with the unforeseen. Complete strangerhood may abnormally loosen or radically undermine normal restraints on behavior.

The reasonable have no enemies.

Confucius said, "If you are exacting with yourself while forgiving to others, then you will put enmity at a distance."

One should not reveal one's own weakness.

In terms of strategic science, to reveal one's own weakness is to make oneself vulnerable. The energy then spent on remedial defense is not available for constructive action.

It is the patient one who sees everything through.

Confucius said, "Those whose strength is insufficient give up along the way."

Money should be saved for hard times.

Among the fundamental management principles adopted by the Japanese industrial magnate Matsushita Konosuke, one of the most successful businessmen of the twentieth century, was to maintain a thick cash cushion, a specific level of reserve established to keep the enterprise operating effectively through difficult periods.

Do tomorrow's task today;
do the afternoon's in the morning.

The *Tao Te Ching* says, "Do it before it exists; govern it before there's disorder."

Morality conforms to convention.

The ethical evaluation of an action depends on the agreements informing the system of values. When different systems of values are compelled to interact, they may compete, or conflict, or find common ground, or come to new ways of understanding.

All-knowledge means knowledge of the world.
Even if one has formal learning,
without knowledge of the world
one is the equivalent of an ignoramus.

There is no point in pursuing knowledge that is irrelevant and useless. Without knowledge of the world, the possible relevance and utility of formal learning cannot be established.

~≈≋≋≋~

Application of learning is vision of reality.
Knowledge of reality also illuminates work.

To put learning into practice requires an effective understanding of the actual context in which it is to be applied. Knowledge of objective conditions also makes it clear what is useful and what is possible in a given time and place.

~≈≋≋≋~

There should be no bias in litigation.

In ancient Europe, judges were druids, considered the most just of people. Druids were European equivalents of Brahmins in India, both having descended from a common tradition in remote antiquity. The old Irish legal specialists known as brehons, themselves druids and descendants of druids, were famed for their ability to render decisions so fairly that both winners and losers were satisfied. Accurate and comprehensive knowledge of facts and precedents are emphasized in druidical law, and bias and wrangling are counted among four archetypical elements of folly.

The Huainan Masters said, "Just as a balance is fair insofar as it weighs things impartially, and a plumb line is correct insofar as it determines straight lines impartially, so a ruler who applies the law without personal likes and dislikes can thereby command."

Custom weighs even more than law.

Custom is an original source of law. The Huainan Masters said, "Law derives from justice; justice derives from what suits the community. What suits the community is what accords with the hearts of the people. This is the essence of government. . . . Law does not come down from the heavens, nor does it spring up from the earth; it develops among people."

The soul is witness to a transaction.
The soul, indeed, is witness to everything.

Becoming inwardly conscious of the witnessing soul is an exercise in awareness of motives and actions, for the purpose of enhancement of conscience.

One should not be a false witness;
false witnesses fall into hell.

If conscience is false, there is no way of harmonizing motives and actions with truth and reality, and therefore no way of avoiding perpetual friction, aggravation and overall stress to the whole system.

The elements are witnesses of concealed evils;
one reveals one's own evil.

This may be the fundamental principle behind the story of *The Portrait of Dorian Grey*. Hidden vice may leave social face intact as long as it remains concealed, but eventually a toll is taken on the body and the personality. Buddha said, "Don't underestimate evil, thinking it won't affect you. As dripping water can fill a pitcher drop by drop, a fool is filled with evil even if he accumulates it little by little."

Pious, just, delighting in the welfare of the religious,
able to protect the people,

he who has mastered his faculties is a king.
Let him preserve his own domain,
keeping it under control,
devoted to truth and justice;
having overcome hostile armies,
let him protect the land with justice.

The Taoist Huainan Masters said, "The ancient establishment of rulers was not for the service of their desires. . . . Rulership was set up because the strong oppressed the weak, majorities did violence to minorities, the cunning fooled the simple, the daring attacked the timid, people kept knowledge to themselves and did not teach, people accumulated wealth and did not share it. So the institution of rulership was set up to equalize and unify them."

One in whose domain
the sacred syllable *OM* is chanted by sages
is a king, a yogin,
who is not afflicted by disorders.

Integrity of the cultural fabric of a nation promotes stability and resilience. A combination of political and cultural integrity is difficult to shake. Great leaders of vast heterogeneous empires—Charlemagne, Harun al-Rashid, Tamerlane and others throughout history—have understood the value of intellectual, religious, and other cultural elements in the establishment and maintenance of national polities and international alliances.

One who is protector of the helpless,
refuge for refugees, guide to the lost,
haven for the fearful,
supporter of the disenfranchised,
friend, kinsman, patron, resort,
benefactor, boon, teacher,
father, mother and brother to the world,
that one is a leader.

In olden times, people with inclinations toward leadership could begin by behaving in these ways to the extent of their capacities. As this gradually won other people's affections and loyalties, their capacities for further outreach and uplift would increase in proportion.

Punishment of the bad, reward of the good,
increase of the treasury by proper method,
impartiality to supplicants, preservation of sovereignty:
five are the stated duties of leaders.

It may be useful to note areas where punishment of the bad remains a feature of leadership, but not reward of the good. There is also the question of fair distribution of punishments and rewards, based on deeds and not social status.

Fair taxation is a basic issue every government has to consider from time to time. What does the public get for what it gives, what does the government give for what it gets?

If the subjective desires of a select few are met while the objective needs of many people, even whole communities, are virtually disregarded, then real social stability is impossible, even if a semblance of stability can be temporarily obtained by rigidification.

Preservation of sovereignty ostensibly means readiness to repel invasion, but armed invasion is not the only threat to sovereignty. There are various ways of exerting influence inside another country, open and covert, including influence through institutions devoted to commerce, industry, finance, education and so on. Getting a country so deeply into debt that the amount of revenue that must be devoted to debt service staggers the economy may be another kind of threat to sovereignty, especially when a large percentage of the debt is held by other governments. There may also be certain types of people within any given country or organization whose cooperation could be purchased by outsiders; they are actively sought, and if not found may be deliberately cultivated. Leaders have to be careful about all of these things in order to preserve true sovereignty for their nations.

Indifferent to the drinking goblet,
delighting in virtue,
sharing enjoyment with others,
willing to learn science and willing to fight in war:
these are five characteristics of a leader.

Alcoholic drink was disapproved by Hindus and Buddhists because of the way it diminishes the power of self-mastery, thus eroding the basis of morality.

Self-mastery is considered essential to leadership in Kauthilya's philosophy, and this self-mastery is supposed to be expressed in the moral quality of leadership.

The relationship of the leadership to the social body is a primary example of its moral expression. The Huainan Masters said, "When subjects do not get what they want from their rulers, the rulers cannot get what they seek from their subjects."

Willingness to learn is another mode of pragmatic moral expression. In this context, the term *science* includes natural and human sciences. The willingness of leadership to learn keeps the paths of social progress open.

Willingness to fight to defend the nation also reflects the moral sense of the leadership. Although this may seem to be taken for granted, history shows that some leaders will sell out to more powerful adversaries or abandon their nations in favor of comfortable exile when hard times come.

One thing is to be learned from the lion,
one from the crane, four from the cock;
five things are to be learned from the crow,
six from the dog and three from the donkey.
When a man wants to do a task, great or small,
let him do it with all dispatch:
this is called the one thing learned from the lion.

The Taoist philosopher Lao-tzu speaks of doing the great while it is still small, even of doing things before they exist. The sooner something needing attention is taken care of, the less room for further complications to develop and the more energy available for constructive action.

Controlling his senses, the wise man is like a crane;
let him accomplish all tasks by knowing
the potency of the place and time.

Knowing the potency of the place and time means seeing what is actually possible, and when. Control of the senses enables one to have the clarity of mind to attain and utilize this perception. Thus avoiding random action, one can channel energy with optimum efficiency.

Rising early, fighting, sharing with kin
and enjoyment of the fruits of one's own efforts:
these four should be learned from the cock.

Rising at daybreak is a basic way of attuning the individual body to
the solar season. This allows a maximum use of daytime energy throughout the year.

Fighting means being able to defend oneself and one's family, neighbors, community and so on. This was one way that people on the path
of chivalry came to be leaders of nations.

Sharing with kin affirms the original sense of relatedness from which
social contracts arose.

Enjoyment of the fruits of one's own labors confirms meaning in work.
Muhammad the Prophet said that there is no better food than that earned
by one's own labor; and he also related that David, the Hebrew king,
never ate any food but what he earned by the work of his own hands.

Privacy in sex, boldness, timely withdrawal,
vigilance and wariness: these five
should be learned from the crow.

On one level these five are particularly apt for warriors, but they also apply to other people as well, according to the different contexts of their lives.

Privacy in sex is not only simple decency, but also an essential aspect of real intimacy.

Boldness is ability to take initiative and act with alacrity and decisiveness.

Timely withdrawal is ability not to go too far or rely too much on boldness alone.

Vigilance is necessary to watch the timing of events and actions, the changing conditions and the ongoing consequences.

Wariness is that part of watchfulness devoted to preventing trouble before it happens, thus saving energy for other constructive or creative activities.

Desiring much yet content with little,
sleeping deeply yet quick to awake,
loyal and brave:
these are the six virtues of canines.

Desiring much stimulates progress, while contentment with little eliminates aggression. Sleeping deeply promotes rest and restoration; being quick to awake promotes clarity of mind. Loyalty implies a sense of duty; Confucius said that to see one's duty and not do it implies a lack of bravery.

Even when exhausted he will bear a burden,
not minding heat and cold, always going along content:
these three things should be learned from the donkey.

Sometimes there is frustration, but that need not keep one from
working. Sometimes there may be a lot of pressure, and sometimes there
may be slumps, but that need not dominate the mind. One may wish for
anything, but not everything is possible; knowing what is enough protects the soul from wear and tear.

The sagacious one who practices
these twenty verses set forth here
will overcome all adversaries
and remain invincible.

It is not only the individual qualities described, but the whole range
of their combinations that gives rise to the potency here attributed to
them.

Replanting the uprooted, gathering the flowering,
strengthening the weak, lowering the overgrown,
dividing up the superabundant, loosening the compacted,
removing sharp thorns, protecting spontaneous growth:
one who is like a gardener, skilled in undertakings,
remains long in sovereignty.

These seem to be perennial tasks of government, in whatever form: resettlement of the disenfranchised, fair taxation of profits, assistance of the needy, regulation of growth, prevention of monopolies, elimination of congestion, isolation of criminals and education of the young.

Designs conceived by the hostile
are as if divinely thwarted;
the leader who stands on the straight path
is naturally blessed.

The Huainan Masters said, "Anything can be overcome except the Way."

A virtuous quality in a leader,
and in a minister,
is one by which state finances are improved.

The Huainan Masters said, "What is to be done for prosperity today, and what is to be done for justice tomorrow—this is easily said. What is to be done for justice today, and what is to be done for prosperity tomorrow—this is hardly known."

One who spends irrationally,
one who is argumentative,
one who is sickly
and one who consumes everything,
quickly perishes.

Irrational spending leads to financial ruin. Contentiousness leads to hostility. Sickliness leads to isolation. Overconsumption leads to lack.

Better to have no country
than a country with a bad ruler.
Better to have no friend than a bad friend.
Better to have no student than a bad student.
Better to have no wife than a bad wife.
How can there be happiness in a badly ruled country?
How can there be solace in the friendship of a bad friend?
How can there be enjoyment in a home with a bad wife?
How can there be honor in teaching a bad student?
There is no trusting a bad friend,
no enjoying a bad wife;
there is no tranquility in a bad kingdom,
no life in a bad place.

Social order, friendship, family and education all influence the quality of life.

Clothed in armor, fierce, proceeding indirectly,
hooded, yet susceptible to direction,
rulers are like snakes.

The armor of a ruler is organization; the ferocity of a ruler is ambition; the indirectness of a ruler is tactical diplomacy; the hood of a ruler is delegation of authority; a ruler's acceptance of direction is consultation.

The root of law and order is the leaders,
and the root of sacred lore is the learned.
Where the learned are respected,
there law and order is everlasting.

The learned are respected where cultural values are honored and their integrity is maintained. Because cultural values inform customary law and social order, common respect for these values is the primary force that maintains law and order.

One who gives up his own kind and takes to another
goes to his own dissolution,
as does a leader by following an alien rule.

Confucius said, "Those whose paths are not the same do not consult each other."

Sovereignty and success, status and purity,
erudition, longevity, and health—
this is the fruit of justice.

The concept of justice had broader meaning in ancient philosophies than it does in common usage today. Socrates said, "It is by justice that the universals of the world exist, and its particulars cannot exist without it." Here in Kauthilya's aphorism, justice appears to imply fairness in professional conduct, fairness in social relations, fairness in respect for truth, and fairness in employment and treatment of the body. The aphorism does not suggest, however, that the beneficial results of justice are themselves the aims of fairness; it only says these are effects of justice. Confucius said, "Cultivated people understand things in terms of justice; small people understand things in terms of profit."

He protects the country,
always devoted to true justice;
having overcome enemy armies,
let him provide security
as is right for a lord.

The leadership of an entity such as a nation or a corporation can effectively lead only if it can keep the entity together by maintaining the internal integrity of its operation while protecting it from external threats.

A leader who gets angry at a minister for no reason
will be maddened by venom, as if bitten by a cobra.
A leader should not frown
or get angry without reason;
when they are not at fault,
the leader should protect ministers with justice.

Arbitrary behavior arousing resentment can have serious consequences within an executive group whose effectiveness at the head of an enterprise requires sincere cooperation. The reverberations of random disruptions can drive people to distraction.

What is strange about a learned man
versed in sacred lore becoming a sage?
What is strange about a just man
adroit in political science becoming a leader?

It may be assumed, particularly today, that attainment of positions of leadership comes about only through personal ambition and desire for power. That would seem to rule out the possibility of truly impartial justice. It might happen, however, that honesty, intelligence and knowledge could achieve leadership naturally, without selfish ambition or drive, as naturally as the learned might become wise. The contrived and the natural way would produce two different kinds of candidate; we are asked to question ourselves *why* we would expect one kind more than another.

❦

It is a wonder when a beautiful young girl
becomes a chaste woman;
it is a wonder when a man tormented by poverty
does nothing wrong at all.

Sociological approaches to the problem of crime date back more than two thousand years in China as well as in India. The Taoist Huainan Masters said, "No one has ever heard of anyone who avoided breaking the law and risking punishment when both hungry and cold."

The helpless, the poor, the young, the old,
the distressed, the unjustly slighted—
a leader is the refuge of them all.

The followings of prophets and revolutionary leaders all over the world have swelled with people whose needs have been forgotten or disregarded by the existing order.

The leader is the strength of the powerless,
crying is the strength of infants;
silence is the strength of imbeciles,
falsehood is the strength of thieves.

For masses of the individually powerless, unification and organization make it possible to attain great power.

For Taoists the ability of infants to cry all day without getting hoarse is an example of the potency of naturalness.

For fools there is wisdom in not voicing folly.

For thieves there is nothing more important than deceiving the eye, ear, thought and attention of those around them.

The leader's wife, your teacher's wife, your friend's wife,
your wife's mother and your own mother—
these five are thought of as mothers.

That is, these people are respected as if they were one's own mother.

A prostitute will desert a man gone broke,
people will abandon a defeated leader;
birds will abandon a tree whose fruit is gone,
and guests will abandon a house after eating.

This seems to be a reminder that if you find that you suddenly acquire a lot of "friends" when you have become successful, you may or may not care to determine whether they like you for who you are or for what you have.

The leader should amass wealth justly on the one hand,
while on the other should use that to foster
the finest freemen.

When revenue is invested in the development of human resources,
the resulting increase in productivity will also increase revenue. The
developmental cycle can then be repeated on a progressively larger scale.

Even incompetent ascetics accumulate material goods;
so why not protectors of the earth,
on whose resources the people depend?

Wealth is not the goal of leadership itself, but it is a means of exe-
cuting the obligations and responsibilities of leadership.

Momentary success is hard to gain;
once gained, it can fulfill human needs.
If it is not put to good use here,
when will this opportunity ever occur again?

Wealth is valued for what can be attained and accomplished by the means it affords. One who only hoards wealth and does not put it to good use cannot obtain the full benefit of wealth.

It is true that pleasures delight the mind,
it is true that enjoyments are powerful;
but life is inconstant,
unsteady as the stagger of a drunken woman.
Having attained momentary affluence,
set your mind on permanent truth;
for success vanishes in a moment,
along with oneself.

The impulse to consume one's success can be balanced by recollecting the transitoriness and frailty of conditional things, including the

world and the human body. This realization lends balance and sobriety
to the experience of success.

In alliance, in conflict, in almsgiving, in gaining fame,
in self-gratification, even in attaining liberation,
wealth is the leader's ally.
One who has resources has friends,
one who has resources has associates;
one who has resources is a man of the world,
one who has resources is learned.

Assistance, tribute, hospitality, defense, charity, publicity, recreation and education all require resources.

Where does it come from to begin with?
And when it disperses, where does it go?
The way of wealth is inscrutable.

An accumulation of circumstances, events and actions, none of
them anything in itself, can reach a critical threshold, past which a certain

pattern takes shape and repeats itself. The accumulation of a fortune by one person inevitably depends on the actions of countless people, the majority of whom may be unknown to each other and unaware of their part in the making of a fortune somewhere. When a fortune is consumed, by the same token, it dissolves into the environment, eventually passing into the hands of people who know nothing of its origin.

The works of the stupid man who has lost his wealth
all come to an end,
like a stream drying up in the summer heat.
Friends abandon one who has lost his riches;
so do children, friends and society.
They resort to him again when he is wealthy;
so wealth is a man's friend in the world.
Where there is water, swans resort;
when it dries up, they leave.
They resort there again when there's water there.
A man should not be a friend like a swan.

Most classical philosophies on the art of living, if not all of them, recommend mindfulness of the danger of ruin when in the flush of success, to avoid complacency and laziness. The other side of this is responding to adversity with self-improvement, to avoid bitterness and despair. Even if you accept, as a warning and a precaution, that others

may abandon you when you are in difficulty, nevertheless you should not
yourself be one to abandon others when they are in need.

Picking each blossom individually,
without cutting the roots,
be like a gardener in his garden,
not like a charcoal maker.

How to utilize resources without using them up is one of the main
problems of modern civilization.

Milk is enjoyed after milking,
not after slaughtering;
a country is to be enjoyed by rulers
through methods like milking.
The milk of the cow is not obtained
after drying her up;
likewise, tribute is not obtained from a country
by beleaguering it unfairly.

Exploitation of office and excessive taxation are ultimately counter-productive, undermining the bases of wealth in both private and public sectors.

As a bee collects honey from flowers,
so should a ruler take in revenue,
amassing a store.
A country is said to be like honey;
and the honeybees are not to be killed:
a ruler should draw the yield of the earth
and also protect it,
as one would look after a calf.
An anthill, a honeycomb, a waxing moon,
royal riches and charity
increase bit by bit.

Wealth that is obtained gradually, without unfairness or exploitation, can accumulate in relative security. The greater the accumulation, the greater the capacity for altruistic action. When both means and ends are considered acceptable and there is no resentment or opposition toward either the accumulation or the employment of the wealth, then the cycle of growth, distribution and expansion may continue unobstructed, within the limits of environmental conditions, until a natural equilibrium is reached.

Flies seek open sores, rulers seek wealth;
the low seek a fight, the righteous seek peace.

Flies seek open sores to feed on. Rulers seek wealth to support the aims of the nation. The low seek a fight as a way to prevail. The righteous seek peace as a way to prosper.

Read, son; what good is laziness?
One who does not read becomes a porter,
while a scholar is honored royally.
Read, son, every day!
Read, son, always; keep it forever in your heart.
A king is honored in his own land,
knowledge is honored everywhere.
Scholarship and rulership are never equal:
a king is honored in his own land,
the sage is honored everywhere.

Profound respect for learning was characteristic of the great classical cultures of China and India, but this was not peculiar to the East. In classical Ireland, one of the oldest Western cultures, scholars of the highest rank were equal in status and privilege to kings. For centuries after the fall of the Roman empire, many of the teachers of the schools of Western Europe were either Irish or from the Irish tradition.

Scholars were not only more socially mobile than most people, they also had more opportunities for travel. Scholars in ancient China, Ireland, India, Japan and elsewhere would travel extensively as part of their professional training. Courts eager for knowledge of the outside world, meanwhile, seeking knowledge of useful things or techniques, of possible allies, of potential enemies, would normally extend hospitality to learned and skilled people from all over.

Without learning, an individual's horizons would be severely limited in the ancient world. This is still the case in the modern world.

A ruler born blind is better than one without learning;
the blind one sees by means of a scout,
while the one void of learning sees not at all.

In the *Instructions of Cormac,* a classical Irish manual of leadership, kings are advised to encourage the sciences and to learn arts, languages and skills in various kinds of work. Kauthilya also said, "Song, dance, painting, instrumental music, mathematics, practical arts, political economics and the science of archery: the ruler should actively preserve these."

One arrow shot by an archer may kill or not;
but the design of a sage can destroy a country,
including its ruler.

Classical learning included strategic science, which is of most critical importance for rulers in particular. The Taoist Master of Demon Valley said of this science, "Petty people imitating others will use this in a perverse and sinister way, even getting to the point where they can destroy families and usurp countries." Unless it is known and understood, there is no way to develop effective defense against it.

A ruler who has suffered misfortune
should not be anguished;
he should also cut down the ego's success,
and neither be depressed nor elated.

Buddhist thinkers also deemed it wise to consider adversity a good opportunity for development of detachment, critical self-examination and compassion for others.

Those who are self-possessed
do not become depressive,
even in distress;
does not the moon reemerge
after it has been eclipsed?

The caliph and Sufi master Ali said, "Patience comes down according to misfortune; so if anyone strikes his hand on his thigh in his misfortune, his work comes to naught."

A ruler is to be insightful, mild,
free from foibles, inaccessible, sacrificing,
equanimous in hardship and ease.

A leader needs insight to see how to motivate people and restrain them, according to conditions. A leader needs mildness for sympathy and tact, to protect people's feelings and preserve goodwill. A leader needs inaccessibility for professional integrity, to avoid being swayed by private interests of factions, cliques and self-seekers. A leader needs to be sacrificing in consistently placing the interests of the nation or the group above personal preferences. A leader needs to be equanimous in hardship and ease in order to avoid infecting the social, professional or national body with a sense of fearfulness or a sense of complacency.

One should always restrain fickle opinion
and restrain false talk in freemen, priests
and the servant class.

A Zen proverb says, "When one person tells a falsehood, myriad people pass it on as truth." The influences of fickle opinion and false gossip can cause incalculable loss of potential by crippling and distorting common sense and blurring perceptions of reality.

Justice is preserved by power,
knowledge is preserved by application;
a ruler is protected by gentility,
the home is protected by a good wife.

If people are powerless themselves and are not protected by the powers that be, who will give them justice when they are wronged by deceit or by force?

If knowledge is not applied in some concrete way—be it art, ethics, education, manners and customs, technology, law, literature—then it disappears from human consciousness.

If the leadership is harsh and oppressive, it will always have enemies.

If the wife has no interest in home life, a household will break up.

Night rambling is poison;
the favor of a king is poison.
A wife whose heart is with another is poison;
undetected illness is poison.

Night rambling drains energy, by its own nature and by the nature of its various complications.

The favor of a king brings envy, jealousy and the danger of loss of favor.

A wife whose heart is with another is not like a wife.

An undetected illness goes without treatment.

One should sit with good people
and always associate with the good.
Let both debate and friendship be with the good;
do nothing whatever with the corrupt.

One should abide with the learned,
the cultured, those who know what is right,
those who speak the truth—
stay with them even in prison,
rather than rule with mischief makers!
One eye is discernment,
the other is association with the good;
whoever lacks these two eyes
surely soon falls into a pit of delusion.
Who is an enemy, who is a friend?
Who is indifferent, who is impartial?
Who is venerable, who is estimable?
The simpleton who fails to recognize these
is lost everywhere.

Confucius said, "Three kinds of friends are beneficial, and three are harmful. When friends are honest, sincere or knowledgeable, they are beneficial. When friends are pretentious, fawning or opportunistic, they are harmful."

The great Zen master Zhantang said, "The difficulty of knowing people is what ails sages." The famous strategist Zhuge Liang wrote, "Nothing is harder to see than people's natures. Though good and bad are different, their conditions and appearances are not always uniform. There are some people who are nice enough but steal. Some people are outwardly respectful while inwardly making fools of everyone. Some people are brave on the outside yet cowardly on the inside. Some people do their best but are not loyal. Hard though it be to know people, there are ways."

The Sufi master Ali advised, "Do not befriend a fool, for he hurts you when he wants to help you. And do not befriend a stingy man, for he will distance himself from you when he is most needed. And do not befriend a profligate, as he will sell you for a trifle. And do not befriend a liar, for he is like a mirage, making the distant seem near to you and the near seem distant."

Untrained employees, an ill-bred ruler,
false friends and an immodest wife:
these four are painful sorrows,
spikes to the head.

Failure to train employees thoroughly may cost more than it saves in the long run. Position and power may be more easily corrupted without personal cultivation on the part of those who hold them. False friends abuse trust, undermining faith in humanity. An immodest wife compromises the stability of the home by creating questions about its integrity.

A ruler should give up indulgence in diversions;
those who are devoted to pleasure
are manipulated by existing enemies.

Gambling, hunting, women, drink,
touring and slumber—
a king perishes quickly through addiction to these.

According to classical Chinese strategic science, anything that has form can be attacked and overcome. An indulgence, habit or addiction, as a rigidly fixed form, presents a stationary target for poachers, as well as a constant preoccupation of energy.

A man who will rationalize violation
of well-informed convention, of civilized norms,
also perishes quickly,
in this world and the next.

As times change and a society ages and struggles to adapt, people begin to ask themselves what constitutes well-informed convention and civilized normalcy. Taoist philosophers tried to solve this problem by focusing on the sources of conventions and norms, and the reasons why conventions and norms became conventional and normal. That way, they envisioned, stability would not have to be won at the cost of adaptability. The Huainan Masters said, "Whatever is inappropriate in the policies of former regimes is to be abandoned, while whatever is good in the affairs of latter days is to be adopted. There has never been any fixed constant in manners and culture, so sages formulate manners and culture without being ruled by manners and culture." Thus emphasis lies on keeping well informed, in order that norms and conventions can be well formulated.

A king who is pretentious and proud
of his retinue and possessions
is soon overcome by enemies,
at court and at war.

The *Tao Te Ching* says, "Those who assert themselves are not illustrious; those who glorify themselves have no merit; those who are proud of themselves do not last."

Society as a whole is controlled by authority,
for the innocent man is rare.
It is through fear of punishment
that society as a whole partakes of enjoyment.

The Taoist Huainan Masters said, "Now that society's virtues are declining and mores are growing weaker, to want to govern a decadent populace with simple laws is like trying to ride a wild horse without a bit and bridle." They also said, "What restrains and punishes is law. When people have been punished and yet are not resentful, this is called the Way."

An ignorant person is pitiful,
infertility is pitiful,
people without food are pitiful,
a country in anarchy is pitiful.

The Huainan Masters said, "When people have more than enough, they defer; when they have less than enough, they contend. When people are deferential, then courtesy and justice arise. When people contend, violence and disorder occur."

Fortunate are those who do not see
the breakup of the country,
the destruction of the family,
the estrangement of a wife,
the ruin of a son.

These things occur with greater frequency, affecting ever greater numbers of people, as the fabric of a society decays.

Wealth again, a friend again, a wife again, land again— all this can be regained, but not the body, ever again!

The *Tao Te Ching* says, "Which means more to you, your body or your goods?"

One should not stay where five things are not found: worldly means of livelihood, security, modesty, courtesy and morality.

To stay where there is no way to make a living will lead to dependency or crime. Where there is no security, there can be no freedom from anxiety and no peace of mind. Where there is no modesty, courtesy or morality, there is nothing to mitigate interpersonal contention, friction and conflict.

One should abide in a place
where there is abundant respect
and abandon where there is lack of respect.
One should shun even the company of angels
if there is no respect.

When people are not respected, their potential for good is not nour-
ished and enlivened. When people do not respect others, they interact
without deference and consideration, thus creating chronic irritation.

A bad country, a bad custom, a bad wife,
a bad river, a bad friend and bad food—
these are always shunned by the wise.

A result of chronic irritation is unease and illness. One of the ways
to aim for a healthy life overall is to consider the mental and physical
impact of the events, habits, people and things in the environment.

One who stands by in sickness, in calamity,
in famine, in danger from enemies,
at the door of the ruler and at the burial ground,
that is a friend!

Ali said, "A friend is not a true friend unless he protects his brother in three situations: in his misfortune, in his absence and at his death."

Someone who thwarts you behind your back
yet speaks kindly to your face
should be avoided, for such a friend
is a pitcher of poison with milk on top.

When people enjoy being flattered, they may not think of it as a test or as a cover for backstabbing. One of the classic Chinese Thirty-Six Strategies is "Hide a sword in a smile."

Association with good people
is a basis of success, above all;
a grain that has grown to the size of the husk
does not grow anymore.

A Zen classic says, "It was our parents who gave birth to us, our companions who raised us." The caliber of people with whom one habitually associates is the "size of the husk" within which character and potential grow and develop.

Good qualities should be mentioned,
even if they are an enemy's;
faults should be mentioned, even if they are a guru's.
A statement should be accepted if it is reasonable,
not out of respect for a guru.

One of the fundamental principles of Buddhist doctrine is "rely on truth, not on personality." Confucius also said, "A cultured individual does not promote people just because of what they say, nor ignore what is said just because of who is saying it."

A man who wants to trust an enemy
is considered to have gone to sleep up in a tree
and fallen down.
One should not trust a defeated enemy
who has come to be friendly;
a crow sees a burnt-out cave as full of owls,
even when the fire is out.
One should not trust a false friend,
nor trust a friend, for that matter;
someday a friend in anger
may reveal all secrets.
One should not trust the unfaithful,
nor trust the faithful too much;
for when insecurity arises from trust,
it cuts right through the roots.

The Sufi master Ali said, "Do not trust the disaffected."

The remnant of an illness, the remnant of a fire,
the remnant of an enemy and the remnant of a debt:

these can act up again and again,
so one should see to it that no remnant remains.
An enemy should not be ignored by the wise,
even an enemy with little power;
for even a little fire, when it grows,
will reduce a forest to ashes.
Never ignore an enemy
just because you know he is trifling;
in time his maliciousness acts out,
like a spark of fire in straw.

Stopping destructive forces while they are still minimal in power is an example of the Taoist technique of "doing the great while it is still small." In a collection of sayings called "Stopping Gaps," the Taoist Master of Demon Valley said, "When things are perilous, sages know it, and preserve themselves in solitude. They explain things according to developments, and thoroughly master strategy, whereby they discern the subtle. Starting from the slightest beginnings, they work against tremendous odds. What they provide to the outside world, strategies for nipping problems in the bud, all depend on stopping gaps."

One should not be too straightforward.
Go see the woodland: the straight trees are cut down,
while the crooked ones are left standing there.

The *Tao Te Ching* says, "Be tactful, and you remain whole; bend, and you remain straight."

Success is on the tip of the tongue;
friend and kindred are on the tip of the tongue.
Even imprisonment is on the tip of the tongue;
certain death is on the tip of the tongue.
O tongue, you are fond of pungent things;
why not speak sweetly?
Speak sweetly, auspicious one;
this world is fond of sweetness.
Everyone is pleased by a gift of pleasant words,
so that is what should be said;
what poverty is there in speaking?

Ali said, "Speak, and be known, for a man is hidden under his tongue." He also said, "Many a spoken word is more piercing than an attack." Buddha said, "Do not say anything harsh; what you have said will be said back to you. Angry talk is painful; retaliation will get you." The Qur'an says, "Speak nicely to people."

By negotiation, by giving, by division,
by invasion and by power:
by all means is an enemy to be destroyed
by rulers of men at all times.

The *Tao Te Ching* says, "When you make peace between enemies in such a way that resentment is sure to remain, how can that be called skillful?"

An enemy may be fought by means of another enemy
who is obliged for a favor,
just as a thorn stuck in the foot
may be removed by a thorn held in the hand.

In the Thirty-Six Strategies, setting one's own adversaries against each other is called "borrowing a sword to kill another."

The soft are killed by gentle means,
by gentle means the tough are killed.
Nothing is impossible by gentle means,
so gentleness is fiercer.

This is also an essential principle of Taoist life philosophy and martial arts. The *Tao Te Ching* says, "What is softest in the world drives what is hardest in the world." It also says, "A great nation flows downward into intercourse with the world."

A great gathering of people can deflect an enemy;
a rain-bearing cloud can be withstood by grass.
A large number of people, even if individually powerless,
are irresistible when united;
a rope is made of mere straws twisted together,
but with it even an elephant may be tied.

Many means of uniting people are commonly used to tap the power of masses, including convention and custom, organization and order, ideology and education. The Huainan Masters said, "When a group of people unifies, a hundred people have surplus strength. To rely on the power of one individual, therefore, is sure to result in insecurity."

When total destruction occurs
and there is danger to lives,
one should earnestly protect lives and goods,
even by bowing to an enemy.
At certain times, there is alliance with an enemy,
at certain times, there is division with a friend;
the sage awaits the right time, depending on opportunity,
to do what is to be done.
One should carry a foe on one's back
as long as the time is adverse;
then when the time comes, one should destroy the foe,
like smashing a pot with a stone.

Strategy may employ ideology, and may serve ideology, but a strategy does not necessarily reflect an ideology. Certain Asian martial arts are essentially based on the principle and practice of not resisting the strength of adversaries but utilizing it to your own advantage, avoiding destruction and conserving energy in the process. The ability to survive destruction, regain equilibrium, and ultimately prevail by adapting to changing conditions depends upon the capacity to perceive and predict situations and possibilities accurately, and to act in such a way as to effectively make the best of each time and condition.

Do not let another know your own shortcoming,
but know the other's shortcoming;
hide like a turtle withdrawing its limbs,
but observe the other's condition.

Letting others know your shortcomings makes you vulnerable to them. Knowing others' shortcomings helps you make yourself invulnerable to them. Kauthilya also said, "One should conceal one's own vulnerabilities, and consider others' vulnerabilities." When asked how he overcame his opponents, Ali said, "I never met any man who did not help me against himself."

The deed conceived in the mind
should not be revealed in words.
The secret should be preserved in code
and applied in action.

Security is one of the cornerstones of planning. Meddlers do not even have to be ill intentioned to spoil plans by their interference.

Only one seeking to accomplish something enters into alliance;
when one's aim is fulfilled, there is no alliance.
Therefore, all works should be done in such a way
as to leave something more to do.

The *Tao Te Ching* says, "To govern the human and serve the divine, nothing compares to frugality. Only frugality brings early recovery; early recovery means buildup of power." If political or professional alliances are pursued in such a way as to exhaust themselves, instability and even enmity can result. The same thing can happen in social and romantic alliances.

Alliance should never be made
for the sake of supremacy or power;
when it's gone, there's no respect,
and when it's there, it consumes resources.

Alliances made for supremacy or power may flower at their peak if they do in fact succeed, then sour when their heyday has passed. If you make alliances with others for your own supremacy or power, you may find that others have made alliance with you for *their* supremacy or power.

The covetous may be won over by material goods,
the arrogant by respectful behavior,
the inexperienced by enticement,
and the sage by docility and truthfulness.
The superior should be met with respect,
the powerful with diversion,
the inferior with generosity,
the equal with energy.

One of the capacities of leadership is to recognize different human characters and understand their psychologies. This capacity makes it possible to alter behavior according to type in order to deal effectively with a wide variety of individuals, groups and situations.

One should abandon a law that is void of compassion.

Ali said that an expert jurisprudent "does not cause people to despair of God's mercy."

One should abandon a teacher who is lacking in knowledge.

Ali said, "God does not oblige the ignorant to learn until having obliged the learned to teach."

One should abandon a wife with an angry face.

Pythagoras said, "Sitting on a roof's edge is better than living with a turbulent woman."

One should abandon unfriendly relatives.

Ali said, "Kinship is more in need of friendship than friendship is in need of kinship."

Be attentive to the affairs of others,
be quick to accomplish your own affairs;
be helpful in the affairs of friends,
be energetic in affairs of state.

Confucius said, "Be respectful at home, serious at work, faithful in human relations."

Separation from a loved one,
disgrace of one's people,
unsettled debt, service of a bad ruler
and a friend who turns away from you
because you are poor:
these five things burn the body without fire.

Pining, ostracization, encumbrance, servility and abandonment can lead to nervous breakdown.

Abandon a temperamental boss;
abandon a stingy one even more readily
than a temperamental one.
Even more than a stingy one,
abandon one without discernment.
And even more readily abandon one
who is ungrateful for services rendered.

Work is such an important part of life, materially and mentally, that working for the wrong employer can be among the most stressful and dispiriting things one can do.

Birds abandon a tree whose fruits are gone,
swans abandon a pond that has dried up.
A woman abandons a man of no means,
counselors abandon a fallen leader.
Bees abandon a flower that's lost its freshness,
deer abandon a forest that's been burned.
Everyone has an agenda;
who is appreciative, who is whose beloved?

Understanding the nature of human relations, whether they are based on personal affections, psychological affinities or opportunistic associations, is critical to effective management of social and professional life.

Without associates, no undertakings arrive at success;
therefore, association is the way for a ruler
to go in all endeavors.

The Huainan Masters said, "If you ride on the knowledge of the multitude, it is easy to gain dominion; if you only use your own mind, you cannot even preserve yourself." They also said, "Leaders see with the eyes of the whole nation, hear with the ears of the whole nation, think with the knowledge of the whole nation and move with the strength of the whole nation."

Trees on a riverbank, a lover in other houses
and rulers without advisers—
these quickly go to ruin, without a doubt.
Like trees on riverbanks and loose women,
if a ruler has no advisers, his sovereignty passes away.

Like trees on a riverbank and a woman with no support,
a leader with no counselors does not live long.

Ali said, "There is no backup like consultation."

⸺⚬⚬⚬

Whatever an employee does, good or bad,
increases the merit or demerit of the director.

In Japan, it is considered proper for superiors to take responsibility for the errors of their underlings. There is thus great interest in seeing to it that employees are well screened, well trained and well deployed. Confucius said, "Cultivated people are easy to work for but hard to please. If you try to please them in the wrong way, they are not pleased. When they employ people, they consider their capacities. Petty people are hard to work for but easy to please. Even if you please them by something that is wrong, they are still pleased. When they employ people, they expect everything."

A leader perishes through bad advice,
an ascetic through attachment,
a son through indulgence,
an intellectual through lack of study,
a family through bad children,
morality through association with mischief makers,
women through intoxication,
agriculture through neglect,
affection by absence, friendship by coldness,
affluence by lack of restraint,
and wealth by relinquishment or heedlessness.
A bad woman ruins households,
a bad son ruins the family.
A bad counselor ruins rulers,
a country is ruined by thieves.
Knowledge is ruined by nonapplication,
women are ruined by constant amusement,
a field is ruined by bad seed,
rulers are ruined by the faults
of those in their service.

The *I Ching* says, "Cultivated people consider problems and prevent them."

A physician addicted to drink, an untalented performer,
an uneducated intellectual, a cowardly warrior,
an unpleasant boss, an ignorant recluse,
a ruler surrounded by bad advisers, a troubled country,
a wife who is proud of her youthfulness
and enamored of others:
the enlightened let go of these right away.
A cruel wife, a foolish son,
a messenger unthinking in his words,
unfriendly relatives and peers:
for one who abandons these is great happiness.

Confucius said, "See what people do, observe the how and why, and examine their basic premises."

Employees should be known to be of many kinds,
superior, inferior and middling;
they should be assigned
to correspondingly appropriate tasks.
A ruler should assign workers to appropriate tasks

after having first examined them to see
whether they are superior, middling or inferior.

The Master of Demon Valley said, "If you observe how everyone and everything can be beneficial in some way and harmful in some way, then you can produce excellence in undertakings." The Huainan Masters said, "There are physical and mental limits to what a person can do. This is why someone with one body occupies one position, and someone with one skill works at one craft. When their strength is up to a task, people do not consider it onerous; when their ability suits a craft, people do not consider it difficult."

Employees who are not lazy, who are contented,
who have good dreams when asleep
and who are wide awake when awake,
who are equanimous in good times and bad,
employees who are firm and stable,
are hard to find in the world.
Just as gold is tested by four means—
by rubbing, cutting, heating and beating—
so is a person tested by four things—
by family, conduct, character and work.
Employees may be known as they execute a mission,
kinfolk when calamity comes,

a friend in times of trouble
and a wife when wealth is gone.

Testing people is a critical concern of traditional philosophies of social organization and leadership. The Huainan Masters present a number of practical ways to bring to light the human qualities cited by Kauthilya as parameters of assessment. The test, naturally, differs according to conditions: "There are ways to evaluate people. If they are in positions of high status, observe what they promote. If they are wealthy, observe what they give. If they are poor, observe what they refuse to accept. If they are low in status, observe what they refuse to do. If they are covetous, observe what they will not take. See if they can turn difficulties around, and you can know if they are courageous. Move them with joy and happiness, and you can observe their self-control. Entrust them with goods and money, and you can assess their decency. Shake them with fear, and you can know their discipline."

Between a bad man and a snake,
the snake is better;
a snake only bites at times,
but a bad man with every step.

This applies to both personal and professional life. The classical Zen master Kuei-shan said, "Familiarity with the evil increases wrong knowledge and views, creating evil day and night." Plato said, "Do not befriend evil people, for the most they can give you is safety from them." The Huainan Masters said, "If the wrong people are entrusted with responsibilities, the very nation is imperiled; superiors and subordinates oppose each other, the officials are resentful, and the common people are disorderly. So a single inappropriate appointment means a lifetime of trouble."

When the world comes to an end,
the oceans overflow their shores;
oceans go for a break in the shoreline,
but good people never exceed their bounds.

Ali said, "Contentment is kingdom enough; goodness of character is prosperity enough."

In sages are all good qualities,
while in a fool are bad ones alone;
so a single insightful individual
is better than a thousand fools.

Buddha said, "A fool who is conscious of his folly is thereby wise; the fool who thinks himself wise is the one to be called a fool."

One with good qualities should be employed,
one lacking good qualities should be avoided.
In the sage are all virtues,
in the fool only faults.

Ali said, "Do not befriend a fool, for he hurts you when he wants to help you."

Those who are profound, attentive, soft-spoken,
self-controlled, truthful, capable, aware of what is to be
and knowledgeable of the reality of motivations
mostly become employees of successful,
intelligent pragmatists.

The profound are able to work steadily for long-term goals. The attentive are able to learn readily and seize opportunities. The soft-spoken are able to get along well with others. The self-controlled are capable of great discipline and sacrifice. The truthful are reliable and trustworthy. The capable are productive and effective. Those who are aware of what is to be are capable of efficient planning. Those who know the reality of motivations can tell with whom to collaborate and whom to avoid.

There are three merits for leaders
in employing the wise:
a good reputation, living in paradise
and great enrichment.
There are three disadvantages for a leader
in employing fools:
a bad reputation, impoverishment
and also going to hell.
Therefore, a leader should always employ the virtuous
and avoid the virtueless,
so that justice, pleasure and prosperity may grow.
A ruler should reject employees who are hypocritical,
deceitful, destructive, irresolute and unenthusiastic,
incompetent, and cowardly.
One who is cruel, dissolute, avaricious, irresolute,
tactless, unruly and extravagant
should not be appointed to a position of authority.
One who lacks patience and devotion,
who is rivalrous and greedy,
and who is incompetent and fearful
should be rejected by a leader.

The Taoist Master of the Hidden Storehouse said, "Of all the tasks
of government, none is as great as finding people for public service. To

prepare people for public service, nothing is as good as mastery of political science; and the best political science of all is bringing peace to people.

"As far as the ability to bring peace to people is concerned, generally speaking you will scarcely find 4 or 5 percent of those who have it if you test them by writing. If you test them verbally, you may find 10 or 20 percent. If you test them by psychology, behavior and attitude, you will find a full 80 to 90 percent. This all refers, of course, to a felicitous age with a wise rulership having the clear perception and discriminating choice to make it possible."

A fool should be shunned,
for he is actually a two-footed animal:
he wounds with the arrow of his words,
like an unseen thorn.
In company with a multitude of fools,
whose behavior is animalistic,
all virtues are covered over,
like the sun by clouds.

Buddha said, "If you do not find a prudent companion, a wise associate leading a good life, then journey alone, like a king abandoning a domain he has conquered, like an elephant roaming the forest. It is better to walk alone; there is no companionship with a fool. Walk alone, like an elephant in the forest, with few desires, doing no evil."

An embedded thorn,
a loose tooth
and a bad administrator
are best rooted out.

The Master of the Hidden Storehouse said, "Once you become an administrator, your mind should be impartial, your demeanor should be harmonious and your speech should be correct. Impartiality should not be overbearing, harmonization should not be random and correctness should not be offensive."

A ruler should get rid of a servant who is lazy,
talkative, rigid, cruel, habit ridden,
deceitful, discontent and disloyal.

The Master of the Hidden Storehouse said, "What was pure diligence in perfecting government for service of the nation in ancient times has now become pure diligence in cultivating reputation in service of the self." He also said, "Leaders do not worry about not trusting anyone; they only fear trusting those who cannot handle business."

The Huainan Masters said, "When the directives of the leadership are ignored because of factionalism, and the law is broken out of treachery, and intellectuals busy themselves fabricating clever deceits, and mettle-some men occupy themselves fighting, and administrators monopolize authority, and petty bureaucrats hold power, and cliques curry favor to manipulate leadership, then the ancients would say the nation has perished even though it may seem to exist."

One of good family, morals and qualities,
keeper of all laws, astute, and responsible
should be appointed chief justice.

Confucius said, "Cultivated people understand things in terms of justice. Petty people understand things in terms of profit." Ali said, "An expert jurisprudent is one who does not cause people to despair of God's mercy, does not cause them to lose hope of refreshment from God and does not cause them to feel exempt from the design of God."

A ruler should not be like a subject in actuality,
but people should be like a true ruler.
Just behavior and its opposite in the entire populace
start with the ruler.

The Huainan Masters said, "No one has ever heard of a country being chaotic when individuals are orderly, and no one has heard of a country being orderly when individuals are unruly. If a rule is not straight, it cannot be used to make a square; if a compass is not correct, it cannot be used to make a circle. The individual is the rule and compass of affairs; and no one has ever heard of being able to rectify others while being crooked oneself."

When mother gives poison, father sells son
and government takes everything,
who will be my savior?
Where the ruler is himself a thief,
and so is the minister and the priest,
what shall I do then?
Where protection comes from,
so also does danger come from there.

Danger comes from the same sources as protection because of reliance on sources of protection and trust in them. If a source of protection is corrupted or compromised, the severity of the effect is in proportion to the degree of the reliance and trust that had been reposed in it.

Where the ruler is just, the people are righteous;
where the ruler is bad, the people are bad.
Where the ruler is indifferent, the people are indifferent.
The people follow the ruler;
as is the ruler, so are the people.
The king is responsible for evil done by the people;
the priest is responsible for the ruler's evil.
The husband is responsible for the wife's evil;
and the teacher is responsible for the student's evil.
People are destroyed by a ruler like a lion,
by a minister like a tiger,
by an official like a vulture.

The Huainan Masters said, "In ancient times, under sage leadership, the laws were liberal and penalties easygoing. The prisons were empty, everyone had the same mores and no one was treacherous. Government in later times was not like this. Those above were rapacious beyond measure, while those below were covetous and inconsiderate. The common people were poor and miserable, and they fought with one another. They worked hard but did not achieve anything. Clever deceivers appeared, and there came to be many thieves and robbers."

They also said, "When rulers are very crafty, their subjects are very devious. When rulers have many obsessions and interests, their subjects do a lot of posturing. When rulers are uneasy, their subjects are unsettled. When rulers are very demanding, their subjects are contentious. If you don't straighten this out at the root but concern yourself with the branches, this is like stirring up dust as you try to clean a room, like carrying a bunch of kindling as you try to put out a fire."

The Creator has not given fragrance to gold,
nor fruit to sugar cane, nor flowers to sandalwood;
a scholar is not given riches, nor a ruler long life.
None is wiser than this.

Scholars are supposed to be devoted to knowledge, not to material goods. Rulers are supposed to be devoted to justice, not to an easy life.

Who does not become conceited on acquiring riches?
What materialist has had an end to his troubles?
Whose heart has not been broken by women?
Who indeed is dear to kings?
Who is not within range of time?
What beggar has attained dignity?
Who has gone safely on the way in bad company?

Confucius said, "For those who do not think ahead, there is trouble near at hand."

In the happiness of the people
is the happiness of the ruler;
and in the welfare of the people
is the ruler's welfare.
The ruler's concern is not
his own pleasure and benefit,
but the pleasure and benefit of the people.

The Huainan Masters said, "If leaders can truly love and truly benefit the people, then everyone can follow. But even a child rebels against a parent who is unloving and abusive."

The people help the just one
who is beset by serious trouble.

Ali said, "The first compensation of the insightful and patient one for his understanding and tolerance is that the people side with him against the ignoramus."

This science is all a matter of mastering the senses;
one who behaves otherwise,
without controlling the senses,
will soon perish, even though king of the four quarters.

The *Tao Te Ching* says, "Those who overcome others are powerful;
those who overcome themselves are strong."

Most rulers who are dominated by anger
have been killed by the anger of the people, it is heard;
those who are dominated by lust are destroyed
by enemies and diseases caused by destructive habits.

Rulers dominated by anger are hated for temperamental harshness
and cruelty. Those who are dominated by lust consume disproportionate
time, energy and resources, ultimately draining them of both political
and personal power.

Like an elephant blind drunk driven by an inebriate,
which tramples everything it comes upon,
so does a ruler who is blinded by ignorance
and directed by an unseeing minister.

A large body of people has a lot of power, or a lot of potential, inherent in its mass. Properly channeled, this power can do a great deal of good; misguided, it can do a lot of harm. In his *Book of Family Traditions on the Art of War,* the seventeenth-century sword master Yagyu Munenori, teacher of the Japanese shogun or leader of the military government, wrote, "When those close to the ruler have been after their own interest all along, not acting in consideration of the ruler and thus serving in such a way that the people resent the ruler, when the time comes it is those close to the ruler who will be the first to set upon him. This is the doing of those close to the ruler, not the personal fault of the ruler. It is desirable that the potential for such situations be clearly perceived and that those distant from the rulership not be excluded from its benefits."

A ruler guided by learning
is devoted to the guidance of the people;
he enjoys the earth unopposed,
devoted to the welfare of all beings.

Once when Confucius traveled to a certain state, he remarked to one of his pupils, "How the population has grown!" The pupil asked, "Since they have a large population, what is there to add?" Confucius said, "Enrich them." The pupil then asked, "Once they are rich, what else is there to add?" Confucius said, "Educate them."

The one who breaks his word,
and whose behavior is contrary to that of the people,
becomes untrustworthy
to his own kin as well as to others.
Therefore, one should assimilate,
in conduct, dress, language and customs.

The Taoist classic *Chuang-tzu* says, "Be careful, be prudent, be correct yourself. As far as appearances are concerned, nothing compares to conformity. As far as attitude is concerned, nothing compares to harmony. Nevertheless, there are problems with both of these. When you conform, you don't want to be absorbed, and when you harmonize you don't want to stand out." Confucius said, "Cultivated people harmonize without imitating. Immature people imitate without harmonizing." The *Chuang-tzu* also says, "If by appearing to conform you become absorbed, you will be upset, destroyed, ruined, downtrodden. If you stand out for your interest in cooperation, that will turn into a reputation that will be harmful to you."

One who is loved by the people accomplishes a task
even with little assistance, because of having cooperation.

Someone who is loved by people receives cooperation without asking
for it. Someone who pretends to love people in order to get assistance
may not fare so well.

A self-possessed ruler brings success
to an unaccomplished people.
A ruler who is not self-possessed destroys
a prosperous and devoted people.

A self-possessed ruler has the patience and industry to foster development. A ruler who is not self-possessed lacks the discipline and foresight
to maintain a state of general well-being. A ruler who is self-possessed
leads the people. A ruler who is not self-possessed exploits the people.

An evil-natured ruler,
who governs others even though lacking in self-possession,
will either be assassinated by the people
or be subjugated by enemies.

A ruler who exploits and mistreats the people may be destroyed by their wrath directly, or abandoned to competitors.

The self-possessed one with a loyal populace,
even of a small area, enjoys the earth,
wins and does not lose.

The *Tao Te Ching* describes a realm of self-possessed contentment in these terms: "A small state with few people may have the people keep arms, but not use them. It inspires them to regard death gravely and not go on distant campaigns. Even if they have vehicles, they don't drive them anywhere. Even if they have weapons, they have no use for them. It lets the people go back to simple techniques, relish their food, like their clothes, be comfortable in their ways and enjoy their work. Neighboring states may be so close that they can hear each other's dogs and roosters barking and crowing, yet they have made things such that the people have never gone back and forth."

Whatever the personal conduct of the ruler,
so does the conduct of the populace become.

Confucius said of this phenomenon, "The quality of the leader is like wind, the quality of the people is like grass; when the wind blows, the grass bends."

One who acts at whim, blind for lack of learning,
is either obstinate or pliant.

According to Taoist psychology, an ideal mentality or personality combines firmness with flexibility. Firmness without flexibility to balance it results in rigidity, aggressiveness and obstinacy. Flexibility without firmness to balance it results in weakness, indecision and pliability.

Ignorance and lack of discipline
are causes of vice in a person;

indeed, the uncultivated and unruly
see no ill in vice.
The whole of learning is this:
mastery over the senses.

Ali said, "Captives of desire, desist, for one who is attached to the world is not scared by anything but the screech of misfortune. People, assume your own responsibility for disciplining and refining your selves, deflecting them from their habits."

One who rules by four things—
justice, conventional norms, order and example—
will conquer the four corners of the earth.

The Huainan Masters said, "Law derives from justice; justice derives from what suits the community. What suits the community accords with the hearts of the people. This is the essence of government. . . . When leaders establish law, they personally act as models and exemplars. It is for this reason that their directives are carried out throughout the land. Confucius said, 'When people are personally upright, others go along with them even though they are not commanded to do so; when people are not upright themselves, others will not follow them even if ordered to do so.' Thus when leaders are themselves subject to regulations, then their directives are carried out by the people."

Justice is thwarted by injustice,
a ruler is destroyed by indifference.

The Huainan Masters said, "When sages carry out justice, their concern comes from within—what personal profit is in it for them?"

One should tolerate minor errors
and be satisfied even with a small income.

Tolerating minor errors increases the capacity to keep focused on overall aims. Satisfaction with a small income increases the desirability of work with inherent meaning and reward. By choosing work that is inherently rewarding and focusing on long-term goals, one may attain success and prosperity without anxious ambition.

The action of a leader is based
on direct experience, indirect evidence and inference.

Even direct experience must be examined for authenticity of consciousness, memory and understanding in order to rule out misperception, faulty recollection and illusion; indirect evidence must also be examined for probity of sources; and inference must be examined for soundness of reason.

A ruler who is hard to get to see
is induced by those around him to do the opposite
of what should or should not be done.

Yagyu Munenori wrote, "Surrounding rulers are treacherous people who pretend to be righteous when in the presence of superiors yet have a glare in their eyes when they look at subordinates. Unless they are bribed, they present the good as bad, so the innocent suffer and the guilty gloat. To see the potential for this happening is even more urgent than to notice a concealed scheme."

All urgent tasks should be attended to and not overlooked;
something that has gone too far becomes difficult
or even impossible to take care of.

The *Tao Te Ching* says, "Plan for difficulty when it is still easy, do the great while it is still small. The most difficult things in the world must be done while they are easy; the greatest things in the world must be done while they are small."

Sovereignty can be accomplished
only with assistance;
a single wheel does not move.
One should have advisers, therefore,
and listen to their opinion.
One who does not have the power of magical formulas
should attend people of wisdom
or associate with those advanced in knowledge;
thus does one obtain superior access.
Indra's circle of counselors
consists of a thousand sages; this is his eye.
Therefore he is said to have a thousand eyes
even though he has only two.

The Huainan Masters said, "The abilities of one man are not sufficient even to govern a single household. But follow the measures of true reason, based on the nature of the universe, and the whole world is equal." They also said, "If you ride on the knowledge of the multitude, it is easy to gain dominion; if you only use your own mind, you cannot even preserve yourself." Ali said, "Consultation is a source of guidance, and one who thinks his own view is enough runs a risk."

Which shall it be, one who likes you
or one whom you like?
Go to one who likes you;
that is the best way of alliance.

Someone who likes you is a better choice of allies than someone whom you like because his loyalty to you will not be inspired by your liking him the way it will be inspired by his liking you.

One with increased power, however,
is not to be trusted;
for prosperity is a changer of minds.
Indeed, hardship produces firmness of friendship.

Changes in circumstance may provoke reevaluation of alliances. Considering this may happen, it is important to observe the influence of conditions on the mentalities and attitudes of associates and friends.

READER/CUSTOMER CARE SURVEY

If you are enjoying this book, please help us serve you better and meet your changing needs by taking a few minutes to complete this survey. Please fold it & drop it in the mail.

Name: _____

Address: _____

_____

Tel. # _____

As a special **"Thank You"** we'll send you exciting news about interesting books and a valuable Gift Cerificate.
It's Our Pleasure to Serve You!

(1) Gender: 1) ____ Female 2) ____ Male

(2) Age: 1)____ 18-25 4)____ 46-55
2)____ 26-35 5)____ 56-65
3)____ 36-45 6)____ 65+

(3) Marital status:

1)____ Married 3)____ Single 5)____ Widowed
2)____ Divorced 4)____ Partner

(4) Is this book: 1)____ Purchased for self?
2)____ Purchased for others?
3)____ Received as gift?

(5) How did you find out about this book?

1)____ Catalog   2)____ Store Display
Newspaper
3)____ Best Seller List
4)____ Article/Book Review
5)____ Advertisement
Magazine
6)____ Feature Article
7)____ Book Review
8)____ Advertisement
9)____ Word of Mouth
A)____ T.V./Talk Show (Specify) _____
B)____ Radio/Talk Show (Specify) _____
C)____ Professional Referral _____
D)____ Other (Specify) _____

Which Health Communications book are you currently reading? _____

(6) What subject areas do you enjoy reading most? (Rank in order of enjoyment)

1)____ Women's's Issues/   5)____ New Age/
Relationships   Altern. Healing
2)____ Business Self Help 6)____ Aging
3)____ Soul/Spirituality/ 7)____ Parenting
Inspiration   8)____ Diet/Nutrition/
4)____ Recovery   Exercise/Health

(14) What do you look for when choosing a personal growth book?

(Rank in order of importance)
1)____ Subject   3)____ Author
2)____ Title   4)____ Price
Cover Design   5)____ In Store Location

(19) When do you buy books?

(Rank in order of importance)
1)____ Christmas
2)____ Valentine's Day
3)____ Birthday
4)____ Mother's Day
5)____ Other (Specify _____

(23) Where do you buy your books?

(Rank in order of frequency of purchases)
1)____ Bookstore   6)____ Gift Store
2)____ Price Club   7)____ Book Club
3)____ Department Store   8)____ Mail Order
4)____ Supermarket/   9)____ T.V. Shopping
Drug Store   A)____ Airport
5)____ Health Food Store

Additional comments you would like to make to help us serve you better.

_____
_____

Thank You !!

FOLD HERE

BUSINESS REPLY MAIL
FIRST CLASS MAIL PERMIT NO 45 DEERFIELD BEACH, FL

POSTAGE WILL BE PAID BY ADDRESSEE

HEALTH COMMUNICATIONS
3201 SW 15TH STREET
DEERFIELD BEACH, FL 33442-9875

Assistance is a sign of a friend.

Assistance has many forms. Muhammad the Prophet said, "Help your brother, whether he be an oppressor or one of the oppressed." People asked, "We help him if he is oppressed, but how can we help him if he is an oppressor?" The Prophet said, "By stopping him."

Familiars take over everything
and act is if they were in charge.
Classmates, even if trustworthy, are disrespectful
because of having been playmates.

Delegating authority arbitrarily to familiars by assumption, by association, by mistake, by accident or by default may lead to damages even beyond those caused by consequent bungling and incompetence, through systemic deterioration caused by general loss of faith and confidence in the prevailing order.

Those who are alike in ways
that have to be kept private secrets,
having the same habits and vices,
avoid causing offense out of fear
that their vulnerabilities are known.

Such people can therefore not be relied upon for objective views, forthright opinions or criticism, even if constructive.

Spies should be killed, using the bait of trust,
trapping them when they swallow it.
One should not let enemies pretending friendship
thrive at one's expense.
A clash between equals results in destruction of both,
like unfired pots smashing each other.

Spies can be nullified by disinformation if they can be induced to believe it. Enemies posing as friends can be identified in a time of trouble. Invincible warriors are those who know how to win at minimum cost and know how to choose when to fight.

An army returning to engagement without hope of life
gives rise to irrepressible force;
so do not harass a broken army.

Sun Tzu said in *The Art of War,* "Do not stop an army on its way
home. A surrounded army must be given a way out. Do not press a des-
perate enemy. These are rules of military operations." Mei Yaochen
explained, "Under these circumstances, an opponent will fight to the
death. An exhausted animal will still fight, as a matter of natural law."

By day, the crow kills the owl;
at night, the owl kills the crow.
On dry land, a dog tears a crocodile to pieces;
in the deep, a crocodile tears a dog to pieces.

A particular capacity is not of fixed value in itself; its value depends
upon the conditions under which it is employed. In a diverse environment, a variety of abilities can find domains of successful expression.

In a fight between a dog and a pig,
the ultimate victory belongs to the butcher.

It is for this reason that many a fight has been fomented by many a
meat merchant. The message to people involved in a fight is to examine
their situation and see whether they might not be in the position of the
pigs and dogs, with third parties standing by waiting to butcher their
remains. This might save them energy and keep them whole.

In indolence is certain loss
of what has been gained and what is to come;
results are obtained by action,
and so success is gained.

Consuming without producing uses up results of past efforts and
provides nothing for future needs.

Wealth, justice, pleasure:
these are three kinds of aim.
It is best to gain them in order.

When immature youths come to expect adult pleasures before they are able to assume adult responsibilities, they may grow up into imma- ture and irresponsible adults.

Since it is the root of justice, and pleasure is its friend,
the attainment of wealth linked to justice and pleasure
is the attainment of all aims.

Wealth may be used to support the securing of justice and pleasure for oneself as well as others, but attainment of wealth without justice or enjoyment does not improve the quality of life. With no constructive aim, pursuit of wealth is reduced to blind ambition or obsession, doomed in that sense to failure even in success.

A king with few reserves devours
both urban and rural populations.

Habitual deficit spending by authorities reduces the proportion of
tax revenues available for public works and thus erodes the population's
enjoyment of its own productivity.

Men of no means do not attain their aims,
even by hundreds of efforts.
Objectives depend on material resources,
like elephants herded by elephants.
A kingdom with depleted resources, even if gained,
only becomes a liability.

Ali said, "Form partnerships with those who have abundant income,
for they are fitter for wealth and better suited to its reduction."

Revenue should be collected from a kingdom
like fruit from a garden, when ripe;
doing so in a way that would cause resentment
should be avoided,
as it brings danger of self-destruction.

The Huainan Masters said, "Unprincipled rulers take from the people without measuring the people's strengths; they make demands on their subjects without assessing how much their subjects have."

Just as fish swimming in water
cannot be detected drinking the water,
appointees in charge of works
cannot be detected misappropriating funds.

The Huainan Masters said, "When society is orderly, the common people are upright and cannot be seduced by profit. When society is disorderly, the elite are villainous and cannot be stopped by the law."

Even the course of birds
flying in the sky can be discerned,
but not the course taken by appointees
who conceal their true condition.

The Huainan Masters said, "If the ruler is truly upright, then honest people are entrusted with affairs, and the treacherous go into hiding. If the ruler is not upright, then evil people achieve their aims, and the trustworthy go into concealment."

Even if one is not a thief,
one who happens to be seen on the scene of a theft
will be arrested on account of dress, armament
or accoutrements like the thief,
or on account of proximity to the stolen goods.

Circumstantial evidence may not be admissible in court, but it can still be persuasive, or at least cloud minds. Remembering this fact of life is part of prudence.

Employees paid in milk will kill the calves.

Killing the calves results in more milk at first, then less milk later, from fewer cows. This may be taken as a colorful warning about sacrificing long-term development on account of greed for short-term gains.

There is no corrupting one who is not corrupt,
like water treated with poison;
sometimes a remedy cannot be found for the corrupt.

Buddha said, "One without a wound on the hand may remove poison by hand; the poison will not get in where there is no wound. There is no evil for one who does none."

The steadied intelligence of the resolute, once polluted,
will not return until it has come to an end.

Polluted intelligence will not be purified until the defects of pollution become evident. The *I Ching* says, "When you come to an impasse, change; by changing, you get through."

⁂

When a lot of money has been stolen,
proof of even a small part in it
means liability for all of it.

While the individual profit from a crime is reduced by collaboration with others, individual liability for crime is increased by the actions of collaborators. With the cost of failure far greater than the reward of success, the risk outweighs the advantage. Those who cannot be restrained by social conscience or moral principle may thus take a lesson from calculation.

⁂

To the extent that a ruler divulges
dangerous secrets to people,
to that extent, by that act,
the independent one becomes subject to control.
The works of the unguarded,

even if exceptionally successful,
will undoubtedly come to naught,
like a broken raft on the ocean.
One who is given to carelessness,
intoxication, talking in his sleep or sensuality,
or who has been relegated to obscurity,
or treated with disrespect, betrays secrets.
Betrayal of secret plans causes insecurity in the ruler
and the people dependent on him.
Love and hate, joy and sorrow, resolve and fear:
the wise conceal their secrets
by contradictory expressions and gestures.

The Master of Demon Valley said, "Sages sometimes open up in an evident manner; sometimes they are closed and secretive. They are open to those with whom they sympathize, closed to those with whose truth they differ. As to what will do and what will not, sages examine and clarify people's plans to find out if they are in harmony or at variance.

"Whether they separate or join, there is that which sages maintain; so they first go along with the aims of others: then when they want to open up, they value thoroughness; and when they want to shut down, they value secrecy. Thoroughness and secrecy are best subtle, for then they are on the trail of the Way. Opening up is to assess people's feelings; shutting down is to make sure of their sincerity."

In all cases of a suit concerning marriage or inheritance,
professional rivalry, enmity of peers,
establishment of standards for religious ceremonies,
or association, or other legal disputes,
anger is the foundation and cause of injury.

In the classical legal tradition of Ireland, which was related to the Hindu law of India, angry pleading is called one of the "three doors of falsehood," quarreling is one of "three things that make the wise foolish," contention is one of "three signs of folly" and bitterness is one of "three things that show a bad man."

A case in dispute has four elements:
the law, the procedure, customary usage
and government decree.
The last of these can override the former.
The law is based on truth,
the procedure is based on witness,
customary usage is based on the community,
government decree is based on the ruler's authority.
In a case where a customary norm is violated,

according to established order or legal canons,
the case should be decided on the basis of justice.
Where a rule is contradicted by the logic of justice,
let logic be the authority:
there a written text is invalid.

Every human organization, it seems, has a body of rules, whether written or otherwise; established ways of monitoring events and maintaining order; conventional habits of thought and behavior; and some form of leadership or authority. If there is so much concern for the formalities of the system that new realities cannot be accommodated, then the logic of justice may be sacrificed in its own name.

What is right and meaningful should be taught,
not what is wrong and meaningless.

There are many differences in what is considered right and meaningful or wrong and meaningless, according to time, place and people. Comparing them to see what is universal and what is particular may yield certain insights into human nature and human conditions.

One severe in punishment will be feared by the people.
One mild in punishment will be looked down upon.
One who punishes appropriately will be honored.
Well-informed criminal justice
concentrates the attention of the people
on legitimate aims and desires.
Wrongly inflicted punishment
coming from whim, anger or ignorance,
outrages even renunciants living in the forest;
how much more so householders!
Lack of criminal justice results in the rule of fishes:
without the containment of criminal justice,
the powerful devours the weak.
People of all classes and stages of life are protected
by the ruler's system of criminal justice;
devoted to their own duty and occupation,
they function in their own spheres.
As the root of discipline, criminal justice
brings security to the people:
for youths regarding the dispenser of punishment
as occupying the position of the king of death
do not commit crimes.
Rulers who execute criminal justice
eliminate crime among the people

and bring security.
Criminal justice keeps the world whole,
this world and the next world,
when applied by the ruler according to the crime,
whether to his own son or to an enemy.

Zhuge Liang wrote in *The Way of the General*: "Rewarding the good is to promote achievement; penalizing wrongdoers is to prevent treachery. It is imperative that rewards and punishments be fair and impartial. When they know rewards are to be given, courageous warriors know what they are dying for; when they know penalties are to be applied, villains know what to fear. Therefore rewards should not be given without reason, and penalties should not be applied arbitrarily. If rewards are given for no reason, those who have worked hard in public service will be resentful; if penalties are applied arbitrarily, upright people will be bitter."

When weaknesses are eliminated,
there are no guilty people;
but when guilty people are removed,
weaknesses can still spoil others.

Inhibiting criminal or antisocial behavior is one thing; eliminating the psychological bases of such behavior is another. The Huainan

Masters said, "When laws are set up and a system of rewards is established, and yet this cannot change the mores of the people, it is because this does not work without sincerity."

Those who are impartial to all beings and are trustworthy are liked by the people.

Buddha said, "One who is harmless to all living beings is called noble." Muhammad the Prophet said, "There is a reward for your treatment of all living beings."

Fact should be heard from actual eyewitnesses.

Fact must be distinguished from hearsay before accurate judgment and effective action are possible.

Causes of popular discontent:
Not giving what is due, inflicting what is not due.
Not punishing the guilty, violently punishing the innocent.
Imprisoning those who do not deserve it,
not arresting those who should be taken into custody.
Suppressing righteous customs.
Cleaving to injustice and impeding justice.
Doing what shouldn't be done,
leaving necessary tasks unrewarded.
Offending the noble, dishonoring the respectable.
Hostility to elders, unfairness, cheating.
Not reciprocating favors, not fulfilling promises.
Doing what is not profitable,
thwarting what is profitable.
Not providing protection from thieves
and enriching oneself.
Undermining manly efforts
and impugning the merit of works.
Ridiculing the good while being kind to the corrupt.
Unprecedented acts of violence and injustice.
Suppression of established wholesome customs,
pursuit of iniquity and prevention of justice
result in impoverishment, covetousness
and antipathy among the people.

Ruination of welfare and security
through negligence and laziness on the part of the ruler
results in impoverishment, covetousness
and antipathy among the people.
When impoverished people are desirous,
they become disaffected;
the disaffected go over to an enemy
or assassinate the ruler themselves.

Popular discontent compromises general security within and without, undermining internal strength while increasing danger from external pressures. Therefore, issues of justice are not merely abstract moral questions of human nature; they encompass all the concrete, practical matters of everyday life at every level of social organization, from individual and family to nation and state.

Groups are unassailable to others by virtue of cohesion.

The things that foster popular discontent are unwholesome and ruinous in themselves as they are, and yet they are even more so through their damaging effect to the cohesion of the social fabric. Betrayal of trust, for example, in whatever form it occurs, has particular results according to the nature of the trust that has been betrayed; in addition to that, it also fosters general loss of trust, which in its time causes an even more extensive range of destructive effects.

Like worm-eaten wood, an undisciplined royal family
breaks as soon as it is put under pressure.

Many royal families have crumbled after a few generations; few have maintained power for centuries. A proverb says that the discipline of a family can be seen in its third generation.

One who knows the workings of the world should cleave
to a ruler who has self-control, wealth and subjects,
in a way that is pleasing and beneficial.
One may cleave to someone without wealth or subjects,
but not someone without self-control;
for one without self-control
will not attain great sovereignty,
even if he inherits it,
because of his disregard for practical philosophy
and his association with useless people.

The Huainan Masters said, "When political leaders ruin their countries and wreck their lands, themselves to die at others' hands, a laughingstock of all the world, it is invariably because of their desires."

A fire may burn part of the body, or all of it;
a king can destroy or promote you, family and all.

Employment in the service of the powerful may present the prospect of unparalleled opportunity, but it also carries with it the potential for complete ruination.

One gains security in one's position
by not breaking promises or being contentious.

Breaking promises undermines trust; contentiousness undermines goodwill. One who is not trusted or liked by others will not win cooperation or support, and thus cannot be secure in a position of responsibility.

One should not lose the opportunity
to express the interest of the ruler,

one's own interest, along with the welfare of friends,
as well as the interest of others,
at the right place and time, as long as it is consistent
with what is just and advantageous.

Advocating legitimate interests at appropriate times and places helps to promote social conscience and general fair play. Expressing the interests of others also helps to create a sense of solidarity that enhances the cohesion and morale of the group.

When consulted about works that call for intelligence,
immediate and future, one who is expert
should say what is suitable,
consistent with justice and welfare,
without being intimidated by the crowd.

Those who try to say what they think others want them to say, hoping to curry favor, or who are afraid to say something of which others may disapprove, fearing opposition or dismissal, cannot be reliable informants or advisers in situations that call for independent objectivity.

Those who induce one to be rash, unjust and extravagant,
they are enemies masquerading as friends.

Socrates was asked, "Who is the worst of people?" He replied, "One who helps you follow caprice."

One should deflect horrors from others
and not speak of horrors oneself.

One who neither condones vicious gossip nor engages in it will gain the trust and respect of serious-minded people.

The patient one should endure like the earth
even what is destructive to himself.

Earth is widely used as a symbol of patience, tolerance, endurance and humility. In his *Awakening to the Tao,* the neo-Taoist Liu I-ming wrote, "If people can be flexible and yielding, humble, with self-control, entirely free of agitation, cleared of all volatility, not angered by criticism, ignoring insult, docilely accepting all hardships, illnesses and natural disasters, free from anxiety or resentment when faced with danger of adversity, then people can be companions of earth."

Capable people have been banished
merely because of displeasure.
Even useless people seem dear when they act
in accord with knowledge of desires.

Both employers and employees can use the lesson of this observation, to examine whether rejection or acceptance is based on technical professional criteria or human psychological factors. An ideal work place, no doubt, would demand both professional and social skills on the part of both employers and employees, to combine technical competence with interpersonal harmony.

The wise should always see to self-preservation first,
for those who are dependent on kings
are said to be living in fire.

When asked, one should say
what is pleasing and beneficial;
one should not say what is not beneficial yet pleasing.
What is unpleasant but beneficial
should be said privately,
if the hearer is willing to listen.
Better to answer with silence
than to speak of anything odious.

The Master of Demon Valley said, "Those who speak without seeing what type of person they are talking to will be opposed, and those who speak without finding out the state of mind of the person they are talking to will be denied."

When accomplishments are destroyed,
power is undermined, knowledge is marketed,
rejection is quick, direction is overbearing,
trust is lacking or there is conflict with the powerful,
these are grounds for quitting.

These grounds for quitting all concern things that inhibit creativity, teamwork and productivity. When factors that nullify the worth of effort are found to be intrinsic elements of the structure of a work situation, there may be no remedy but to quit.

Training guides the one with potential,
not the one without potential.

The capacity to discover the potentials of individuals and develop
them accordingly is a mark of an effective system.

Learning can only guide the good listener who is attentive,
who has the discernment to grasp and remember,
and the intelligence to infer and exclude.

Confucius said of his teaching method, "If I bring up one corner, and
the student cannot come back with the other three, then I do not go on."

Just as virgin lumber immediately absorbs
anything with which it is painted,
an innocent mind regards whatever it is told

as authoritative teaching.
Unenlightened teaching is a great evil.

Just as learning requires certain duties, including the exercise of attention, recollection and reason, teaching implies certain responsibilities because of the influence that education has on the psychology and character of individuals and societies.

Discipline and self-mastery are learned
from authorities in the individual sciences.

Generalists and dilettantes ordinarily lack the degree of concentration and expertise found in specialists, and may also lack the degree of general self-discipline needed for mastery of an art or a science. This is why royal courts of olden times, both East and West, traditionally included technical experts and sages of various kinds in their composition.

The learning from which are derived justice and wealth
is the essence of learning of all learning.

This established science, with these established devices,
has been articulated for the acquisition and protection
of this world and the next.
It fosters and protects justice, wealth, and pleasure;
this science destroys injustice, poverty and hatred.

These are the main guidelines for the application of the strategies outlined in this classic: they are properly used to foster and protect justice, wealth, and pleasure, and to destroy injustice, poverty and hatred. This needs to be said for the reason that malpractice of such devices can and does lead to the reverse of the intended effects; it is therefore imperative to examine strategies for their potential effects in context, and exercise reason and conscience in their application.

Wisdom arises from learning, discipline from wisdom
and self-possession from discipline.

Wisdom that arises from learning has a nonsubjective basis. Discipline that arises from wisdom has a noncoercive basis. Self-possession that arises from discipline has an independent basis.

Religious scriptures deal with right and wrong,
economics deals with wealth and poverty,
politics deals with good and bad policies.
Examining logically, philosophy benefits the world,
stabilizing the intellect in both adversity and prosperity.
Philosophy is perennially regarded
as a lamp for all sciences,
a means for all tasks,
a refuge for all religions.

Aristotle said, "Logic is a tool for all sciences."

A state must have people.
Without people, like a barren cow, what is produced?
When there are no people,
there is no community,
and with no community there can be no state.

The Huainan Masters said, "Those who can become rulers must be able to find winners. Those who can win over opponents must be strong. Those who can be strong are those who are able to use the power of other people. To be able to use the power of other people, it is necessary to win people's hearts. To be able to win people's hearts, it is necessary to have self-mastery. To be capable of self-mastery, it is necessary to be flexible."

One who would undertake what is possible
should undertake feasible works;
one who would undertake what is good
should undertake that which is void of ill;
one who would undertake what is auspicious
should undertake that which will result in good.

To plan a successful undertaking, it is necessary to consider the feasibility of the project, the potential for problematic side effects and the predictability of positive results.

Time comes but once to a man who wants time;
it will be hard to get time again when he wants to work.

It is easier to miss a moment of opportunity because of lassitude or lack of inspiration than it is to find a moment of opportunity whenever one happens to feel energetic or inspired.

No one would want physical destruction, even for a huge fortune.

People would not be so inclined to chronic overwork in pursuit of material success if they kept in mind that they were destroying their health for wealth they would not be able to enjoy.

There is success and failure on every path.

Some diplomats and attorneys are more skilled than other diplomats and attorneys. Some teachers and physicians are more skilled than other teachers and physicians. Some plumbers and carpenters are more skilled than other plumbers and carpenters. Some farmers and herders are more skilled than other farmers and herders. Some people may never succeed in anything they try.

Power changes the mind.

Modern psychological experiments designed to study the influence of systematic control over others on the minds of conventionally normal people confirm that power does indeed change the mind; and not, evidently, for the better. In this context, the observation is probably expressed as a warning, to the effect that it is insane to pursue external power without also seeking internal strength to maintain psychological balance and moral integrity.

Like understands like.

Confucius said, "Those whose paths are not the same do not consult one another." The Master of Demon Valley said, "When there is intimacy in spite of distance, that means there is hidden virtue; when there is alienation in spite of nearness, that means there is disparity of aims."

Sons captivated by pleasure do not attack their father.

People who are happy in their own situations do not think of rebelling.

It is courage that repels calamity.

Caution and forethought may not be sufficient to avoid calamity because not all conditions are under anyone's control. Once calamity has befallen, furthermore, cleverness and resourcefulness can hardly be mustered in a crisis without inner fortitude and willpower.

One should go the way that is conducive to welfare.

Profit or position that may seem desirable or advantageous may not translate directly into enhanced welfare if so much attention and energy are consumed by obtaining and securing profit or position that none of their practical benefits can be made available for the general well-being.

There is hardly one among thousands
who can be a leader.

Since leadership requires exercise of greater responsibility than the
average individual has, it must also require greater than average capacity.
The Zen master Huitang wrote, "The way of sages is like sky and earth,
nurturing myriad beings, providing everything. The ways of ordinary
people are like rivers, seas, mountains, streams, hills and valleys, plants,
trees, and insects, each fulfilling only its own measure, not knowing outside of that what is complete in everything."

In vast areas, medicinal plants are found
growing both in land and in water.

Talent may be found in a wide variety of circumstances. The broader
the frame of reference, the more chance of finding people of ability.
Zhuge Liang wrote, "For strong pillars you need straight trees; for wise
public servants you need upright people. Straight trees are found in
remote forests; upright people come from the humble masses. Therefore
when rulers are going to make appointments, they need to look in
obscure places."

One should always associate
with those advanced in discipline
in order to develop discipline,
for that is the root of discipline.

Keeping the company of people who are more accomplished or more developed is a fundamental educational strategy, based on the principle of learning by osmosis as well as formal instruction and informal conversation.

A gambler will keep on gambling,
even at night by lamplight,
even when his mother has died;
and if questioned when in trouble,
he becomes angry.
So the self-possessed one,
who is attentive to elders
and has conquered the senses,
should give up destructive anger and lust,
from which ruin begins.

Being too much under the sway of desires and feelings, without balance and sobriety, results in general heedlessness and irresponsibility, which in turn open the way to many a misstep in life.

A potential cause of distress to the citizenry
should be remedied at once by the alert.

The Master of Demon Valley said, "A gap is an opening; an opening is a space between barriers; a space between barriers makes for tremendous vulnerability. At the first sign of a gap, it should be shored up, or repelled, or stopped, or hidden, or overwhelmed. These are called principles of stopping gaps."

For the sake of a kingdom,
even a father will attack sons,
and sons a father;
how about ministers?

Ali said, "One who has authority is like someone riding on a lion; he is envied for his position, but he knows his situation better."

Even a trivial problem becomes trouble
for one who is beleaguered.

When already on the verge of being overwhelmed, most anything
could become the proverbial straw that breaks the camel's back. Then
again, since great pressure is known to affect one's sense of proportion,
remembering this aphorism might help to reestablish a sense of perspective when relatively minor problems occur in the midst of a larger
crisis.

Like a forest fire,
energy born of difficulty motivates.

It is more constructive and less disheartening to use trouble for motivation than to succumb to bewilderment or a sense of defeat.

No one should be disrespected;
everyone's opinion should be heard.

A sage should make use of a meaningful statement,
even if from a child.

The *Tao Te Ching* says, "Observe yourself by yourself, observe the home by the home, observe the locality by the locality, observe the nation by the nation, observe the world by the world." The Huainan Masters said, "Leaders see with the eyes of the whole nation, hear with the ears of the whole nation, think with the knowledge of the whole nation and move with the strength of the whole nation."

Proper duty is conducive to paradise and eternity;
when it is violated, society will be destroyed by confusion.
One who does one's own proper duty is happy
in the hereafter and in this life as well.

The Huainan Masters said, "No one has ever heard of a nation being chaotic when individuals are orderly, and no one has heard of a nation being orderly when individuals are unruly." They also said, "When society is orderly, the common people are upright and cannot be seduced by profit."

One should enjoy pleasure
without compromising duty or wealth;
then one will not be without happiness.
Indeed, the three are inseparably connected to one another.
Excessive indulgence in any one of them,
be it duty, wealth or pleasure,
hurts that one and the other two as well.

The Huainan Masters said, "The behavior of sage kings did not hurt the feelings of the people, so even while the kings enjoyed themselves the world was at peace."

There is no one without desire.

The *Tao Te Ching* says that sages desire to be without desire; but that is still on account of desire, and is itself a desire.

Wealth escapes the infantile one
who keeps consulting the stars.
Wealth is the "star" for wealth;
what can the stars do?

Wealth may be reliably produced by judicious investment of resources in productive enterprise under suitable conditions; taking a gamble on fortune or luck reflects greed and laziness in the form of wishful thinking.

One with theoretical knowledge but no practical skill
will be disappointed in action.
The fitness of a person is determined by practical capability.

Ali said, "Knowledge is linked to action; so one who knows acts, as knowledge calls for action and will depart if it is not answered."

A steady worker does not stop working
until the job is done.

The *I Ching* says, "Cultivated people persist to the end."

Fire dwells in timber.

With the potential for construction comes the potential for destruction.

What comes of itself should not be disregarded.

Ali said, "Take of the world what comes to you."

The self-possessed one should protect himself.

Confucius said, "They are wise who do not anticipate deception and do not consider dishonesty, yet are aware of them from the start."

One who is wise and self-disciplined should guard himself from his own people as well as others.

People need not be ill intentioned to cause trouble; anyone can make mistakes. Too much reliance on others puts one at the mercy of their shortcomings. Confucius said, "At first, the way I dealt with people was to listen to what they said and trust that they would act on it. Now I listen to what they say and then observe whether they do act on it. This was what was within my power to change."

Calmness and effort are the source of profit and security.

The *I Ching* describes the ideal condition of the individual as "serene and free from agitation, yet sensitive and effective; sensitive and effective, yet serene and free from agitation." Calmness makes it possible to perceive realities clearly; effort makes it possible to act on realities effectively.

Capacity, situation and opportunity foster one another.

Zhuge Liang wrote, "When opportunities occur through events, but you are unable to respond, you are not smart. When opportunities become active through a trend, and yet you cannot formulate plans, you are not wise. When opportunities emerge through conditions, but you cannot act on them, you are not bold."

The leader of a group should be properly benevolent to the group,

well liked, patient, with loyal people
and act according to the collective will.

According to the instructions for kings attributed to the great Irish
high king Cormac, among the qualities of leadership are generosity, affa-
bility, patience, fairness and modesty. Kings are also enjoined to hold
frequent assemblies, a principal method of expressing the collective will
in an ancient form of democracy.

One's own body should be preserved, not material goods;
why care for impermanent material goods?

The Sufi master Ali said, "The man who gets the worst bargain and
is the most unsuccessful in his endeavors is the one who wears out his
body in seeking his wealth but is not assisted by destiny toward his aim,
who leaves the world with his sorrow and pain and arrives at the hereafter bearing his responsibility."

REFERENCES AND FURTHER READING

Citations from parallel literature quoted in the commentaries are taken from the following sources.

Buddhism/Zen

Dhammapada: The Sayings of Buddha. Translated from the Pali, with commentary, by Thomas Cleary. New York: Bantam Books, 1995.

Zen Lessons: The Art of Leadership. Translated from the Chinese by Thomas Cleary. Boston: Shambhala Publications, 1989.

Confucianism/I Ching

The Essential Confucius. Translated from the Chinese and presented by Thomas Cleary. San Francisco: Harper San Francisco, 1992.

The Tao of Organization: The I Ching for Group Dynamics, by Cheng Yi. Translated from the Chinese by Thomas Cleary. Boston: Shambhala Publications, 1988.

Greek Philosophers

Living the Good Life. Translated from the Arabic by Thomas Cleary. Boston: Shambhala Publications, 1997.

Strategy/Military Science

The Art of War, by Sun Tzu. Translated from the Chinese by Thomas Cleary. Boston: Shambhala Publications, 1988.

The Book of Five Rings. Translated from the Japanese by Thomas Cleary. Boston: Shambhala Publications, 1993. Includes *Family Traditions on the Art of War* by Yagyu Munenori.

Mastering the Art of War. Translated from the Chinese and edited by Thomas Cleary. Boston: Shambhala Publications, 1989. Includes *The Way of the General* by Zhuge Liang.

Sufism/Islam

The Essential Koran. Translated from the Arabic by Thomas Cleary. San Francisco: Harper San Francisco, 1993.

Living and Dying with Grace: Counsels of Hadrat Ali. Translated from the Arabic by Thomas Cleary. Boston: Shambhala Publications, 1995.

The Wisdom of the Prophet: Sayings of Muhammad. Translated from the Arabic by Thomas Cleary. Boston: Shambhala Publications, 1994.

Taoism

Awakening to the Tao, by Liu I-ming. Translated from the Chinese by Thomas Cleary. Boston: Shambhala Publications, 1988.

The Book of Leadership and Strategy: Lessons of the Chinese Masters. Translated from the Chinese by Thomas Cleary. Boston: Shambhala Publications, 1992. Contains sayings of the Huainan Masters.

The Essential Tao. Translated from the Chinese and presented by Thomas Cleary. San Francisco: Harper San Francisco, 1991. Contains the *Tao Te Ching/Lao-tzu* and the *Chuang-tzu.*

Thunder in the Sky: On the Acquisition and Exercise of Power. Translated from the Chinese, with commentary, by Thomas Cleary. Boston: Shambhala Publications, 1993. Contains the books of the Master of Demon Valley and the Master of the Hidden Storehouse.

Wen-tzu: Understanding the Mysteries; Further Teachings of Lao-tzu. Translated from the Chinese by Thomas Cleary. Boston: Shambhala Publications, 1992.

INDEX

ABOUT THE AUTHOR

Thomas Cleary received his B.A. summa cum laude in Far Eastern languages from Harvard College in 1972. In 1975 he received his Ph.D. in East Asian languages and civilizations from Harvard University.

Dr. Cleary is a past research fellow of the Center for the Study of Humanities at Kyoto University. He is also an internationally known translator of more than sixty volumes of Buddhist, Taoist, Confucian and Islamic texts from Chinese, Japanese, Sanskrit, Pali, Old Bengali and Arabic.

Reviews of Dr. Cleary's works have appeared in *The San Francisco Chronicle, The Oakland Tribune, The San José Mercury News, The East Bay Express* and *The San Francisco Bay Guardian,* as well as such trade publications as *Nation's Business, Inc., Success,* and *Strategy and Business.*

Books For Everyone

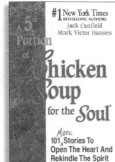

A 5th Portion of Chicken Soup for the Soul

Whether readers are devotees of the series or first-time samplers, they will find this latest serving both riveting and heartwarming. This treasury is a tribute to life and humanity, with topics ranging the emotional and experiential gamut. The nature of the stories invites readers to enjoy *Chicken Soup* in whatever way they find most comforting-by the spoonful, by the bowl, or the whole soup pot in one sitting.
April 1998 Release
Code 5432..........$12.95

Chicken Soup for the Pet Lover's Soul

Like the bestselling *Chicken Soup for the Soul* books, animals bring out the goodness, humanity and optimism in people and speak directly to our souls. This joyous, inspiring and entertaining collection relates the unique bonds between animals and the people whose lives they've changed. Packed with celebrity pet-lore - this book relates the unconditional love, loyalty, courage and companionship that only animals possess.
April 1998 Release
Code 5718..........$12.95

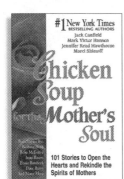

Chicken Soup for the Mother's Soul

We can all remember a time when we were young and under the weather, and Mom soothed and nurtured us back to health with her magical chicken soup elixir. Now we can revisit those cherished moments with a delightful new batch of stories for and about mothers.
Code 4606........ $12.95

Chicken Soup for the Teenage Soul

This batch consists of 101 stories every teen can relate to and learn from—without feeling criticized or judged. You'll find lessons on the nature of friendship and love, the importance of belief in the future, the value of respect for oneself and others and much, much more.
Code 4630................$12.95

Available at your favorite bookstore or call 1-800-441-5569 for Visa or MasterCard orders. Prices do not include shipping and handling. Your response code is WEALTH.

Spiritual Books From HCI

Horse Sense and the Human Heart

In this fascinating book, readers will find that sometimes the best healers are not humans, but Peruvian Paso horses. Amazingly intuitive and responsive, these four-legged therapists bring healing where traditional therapy alone fails.

Code 5238........$10.95

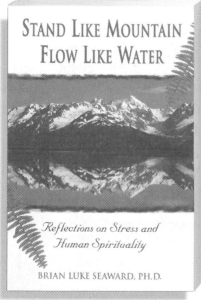

Stand Like Mountain, Flow Like Water

Seaward examines the dynamics of stress, from fight (anger) and flight (fear) to disease. Using the metaphor of the human journey, he explains how stress and human spirituality help nurture the soul's growth process through the use of inner resources, prayer and the seasons of the soul.

Code 4622......$10.95

Available at your favorite bookstore or call 1-800-441-5569 for Visa or MasterCard orders. Prices do not include shipping and handling. Your response code is WEALTH.

Spiritual Books From HCI

The Physician Within You

Dr. McGarey gives readers an exhilarating glimpse of what medicine can be by sharing the philosophy and case histories of her 50-year medical practice. She teaches her patients to access that natural healing process inherent in every human being.
Code 4541......$12.95

Why...

This book will guide readers to discover and appreciate their unique place and purpose, and to see that events that often seem tragic are often to most powerful positive influences on their lives. Norwood comforts readers with stories that reassure them that they are not alone.
Code 522X.........$12.95